CONTENTS

HORNBY MAGAZINE YEARBOOK 8

What's inside...

8 **WEST RIDING POWER: INTRODUCTION**
Mike Wild introduces this year's project layout which has been inspired by a new range of Scenecraft buildings for 'N' gauge.

14 **GROUND COVER TECHNIQUES**
Covering bare baseboards means vegetation as well as structures. Nigel Burkin shows how a variety of materials can be used to create realistic effects.

22 **REALITY CHECK**
The 4-6-0 was a hallmark of British steam locomotive design. Evan Green-Hughes charts development of these go anywhere, do anything engines.

30 **WEATHERING**
Using a pair of pre-nationalisation liveried locomotives Tim Shackleton explores how steam engines looked in the pre-war years.

36 **CARRIAGE LIGHTING**
Adding interior lights to carriages used to be difficult, but not anymore. Mike Wild shows how Train-Tech's battery powered lighting strips can be installed in an LMS inspection saloon quickly and simply.

40 **MAKING A START IN 'N'**
With the growth in popularity and availability of 'N' gauge equipment Nigel Burkin explains how to start out in the scale.

46 **WEST RIDING POWER: POWER AND CONTROL**
Our project layout moves forward as we lay the track, install the wiring and fit point motors to make it all work. Mike Wild explains all.

114 West Riding Power shows how to model power station operations in 'N' gauge.

30 A Bachmann 'D11' and a Hornby '700' illustrate how to weather steam locomotives.

36 We show you how to add carriage lights without any wiring!

78 Scenery breathes life into a model. We explain how we did it for West Riding Power.

54 KEEPING TRAINS MOVING
Layout maintenance is an essential part of railway modelling, especially if you want to get the best from your models. Nigel Burkin shows you how.

60 MASTERPIECES IN THE GALLERY
A host of stunning model railways have featured in the pages of *Hornby Magazine* over the past 12 months. Mike Wild presents a selection of the very best.

72 DIGITAL SOUND
Hornby's Stanier 'Black Five' models one of the best mixed traffic 4-6-0s to be built. Paul Chetter shows how to add to its character by fitting DCC sound, a smoke generator and a 'stay alive' capacitor.

78 WEST RIDING POWER: SCENERY
Developing model railway scenery is a rewarding task. Mike Wild explains how West Riding Power went from bare baseboards to a fully scenic model railway.

86 TRAIN FORMATIONS
Mark Chivers showcases a range of express passenger train formations for 'OO' gauge based on real operations and using readily available locomotives and rolling stock.

94 REVIEW OF THE YEAR
In our annual review of the year Mark Chivers looks back at the highlight new models which made 2015 so enthralling.

106 REALITY CHECK
The BR Type 4 diesel classes were amongst the most successful of the modernisation plan. Evan Green-Hughes explores their story.

114 WEST RIDING POWER: ROLLING STOCK AND OPERATION
Mike Wild explains how the locomotive and rolling stock fleets for West Riding Power has been developed and how the layout works.

122 FORWARD TO 2016
With more than 70 model projects announced there is a lot to look forward to in 2016. Mike Wild charts the latest developments and announcements for 'N', 'OO' and 'O' gauge ready-to-run locomotives.

EDITORIAL
Editor: Mike Wild
Assistant Editor: Mark Chivers
Sub Editor: Andy Roden
Contributors: Evan Green-Hughes, Tim Shackleton, Nigel Burkin, Paul Chetter, Julia Scarlett and Ian Wild.
Senior designer: Steve Diggle

REGISTERED OFFICE
Units 1-4, Gwash Way Industrial Estate, Ryhall Road, Stamford, Lincs PE9 1XP

PRINTING
Gomer Press Limited, Llandysul Ceredigion, South Wales.

ADVERTISING
Advertising: Tom Lee
Email: tom.lee@keypublishing.com
Tel: 01780 755131 **Fax:** 01780 757261
Advertising Production: Cheryl Thornburn
Tel: 01780 755131
Fax: 01780 757261
Email: cheryl.thornburn@keypublishing.co.uk

PUBLISHING
Publisher: Adrian Cox
Tel: 01780 755131
Fax: 01780 757261
Email: adrian.cox@keypublishing.com
Executive Chairman: Richard Cox
Managing Director: Adrian Cox
Commercial Director: Ann Saundry
Sales & Marketing Manager: Martin Steele

Key Publishing Ltd,
Units 1-4, Gwash Way Industrial Estate
Ryhall Road Stamford, Lincs PE9 1XP

SAWYER MODELS

sawyermodelsearlestown @SawyerModels

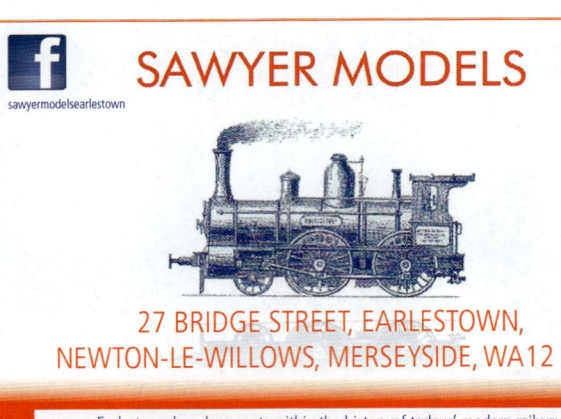

**27 BRIDGE STREET, EARLESTOWN,
NEWTON-LE-WILLOWS, MERSEYSIDE, WA12 9BE**

Earlestown has deep roots within the history of todays' modern railway. Home to the Vulcan foundry where such engines as Deltics and LMS engines were built, the Viaduct Wagon Works where freight wagons were built and more recently, Earlestown has become home to Sawyer Models.

Opened in May 2014, Andrew Sawyer welcomes Loco enthusiasts from across the nation. With a full DCC installed working layout, Sawyer Models provides a great selection for advanced collectors and for those who are just getting started.

Situated on Bridge Street, Sawyer Models are OPEN Monday to Wednesday and Friday to Saturday 10am to 5pm CLOSED Thursdays and Sundays with FREE parking throughout Earlestown and only a 2 minute walk from Earlestown train station.

01925 227835 • sawyermodels@hotmail.com
www.sawyermodels.co.uk

ARC MODELS
4mm scale resin locomotive body kits for R-T-R chassis

Featuring the best names of the industrial railway scene, including;
Andrew Barclay 0-4-0st's and 0-6-0t
Robert Stephenson & Hawthorn 0-6-0t
and coming soon
Bagnall 18" 0-6-0st

I am also looking for keen investor's to help expand ARC Models, with the benefit of lifetime discounts on all products. Please contact me for further information.

For the latest listings and order form, please send a SSAE to the following address;
Mr A R. Cottage
25 St Richards Road
Westergate
Chichester
West Sussex
PO20 3RD
email me at: **arcmodels@fsmail.net**

Or find me on facebook

A *Hornby Magazine* Special Publication
www.hornbymagazine.com

In this brand new Weathering Skills Guide Mike Wild and Tim Shackleton delve into the world of weathering for a second volume offering more than 20 hands on projects, advice for getting started, a buyers guide for airbrushes, essential maintenance. This 132-page special magazine covers all the tips and techniques you will need to develop your own weathered models in scale from 'N' to 'O' gauge and including a wide range of subjects from both the steam and diesel eras.

Features include:
- Airbrush buying guide
- Weathering Hornby's Gresley 'P2' 2-8-2
- Prototype inspirations
- Weathering a Graham Farish Stanier 'Duchess' 4-6-2
- Airbrush maintenance
- Weathering box vans
- Weathering merry-go-round trains
- Weathering freight engines
- Weathering BR blue era locomotives

VOLUME TWO

£6.99 • FULL COLOUR • 132 PAGES

ORDER DIRECT
JUST £6.99 +FREE P&P*
Free 2nd class P&P on all UK & BFPO orders. Overseas charges apply.

Free P&P* when you order online at
www.keypublishing.com/shop

Call UK: 01780 480404
Overseas: +44 1780 480404
Monday to Friday 9am-5:30pm

SUBSCRIBERS CALL FOR YOUR £1.00 DISCOUNT!

Welcome

THE PAST 12 MONTHS have been exciting and enthralling for railway modelling. New models have arrived by the boxload and new announcements have come throughout the year whetting our appetite for more.

The pace of development has shown no sign of abating, and it has been particularly pleasing to see the rate of delivery. Hornby in particular has picked up the gauntlet and released eight new locomotives during 2015, catching up with itself from a rather slower 2014. Dapol too has emerged towards the end of the year bringing out new locomotives in 'N' and 'O' gauges while Bachmann has been especially active in 'N' gauge production.

Long term readers will know that I have a long standing passion for 'N' gauge modelling and even though my primary choice is 'OO' gauge the smaller scale has gained ground both in popularity and with a wider market. This has been echoed by the raft of new releases – there have been nine brand new 'N' gauge locomotives in 2015 – and by the fact that new names are appearing on the scene to develop more for the scale. Revolution Trains is making a strong name for itself with development of its Class 390 Pendolino for 'N' – so much so that it has recently launched two more projects.

Each year the *Hornby Magazine Yearbook* features a project layout and this time it is the turn of 'N' gauge to shine. To create something with a different feel and style, we've moved forward to the 1980s to create a main line scene with a power station as its backdrop – and all in just over 6ft x 4ft, the size of a typical 'OO' gauge train set. West Riding Power has been produced with the support of Bachmann Europe, Gaugemaster, DCC Concepts and Train-Tech.

The result goes to show just what can be achieved in 'N' gauge and with the standard of ready-to-run products being raised with every new release this scale is an ever more viable option for steam and diesel modellers, particularly if you are short of space.

Of course 'N' gauge isn't the only subject of this Yearbook, as the *Hornby Magazine* team has been working hard behind the scenes to deliver a series of brand new features for this book including step by step guides on ground cover, installing lighting in carriages, digital sound and smoke, layout maintenance, weathering and railway history. Not to be missed either is our review of the new releases in 2015 and our look forward to 2016 charting all the models announced for release by the major manufacturers.

We hope you enjoy reading *Hornby Magazine Yearbook No. 8* as much as we have enjoyed putting it together.

Happy modelling!

Mike Wild
Editor, *Hornby Magazine*

CONSTRUCTION OF WEST RIDING POWER IS SUPPORTED BY…

www.gaugemaster.com

www.dccconcepts.com

www.bachmann.co.uk

www.train-tech.co.uk

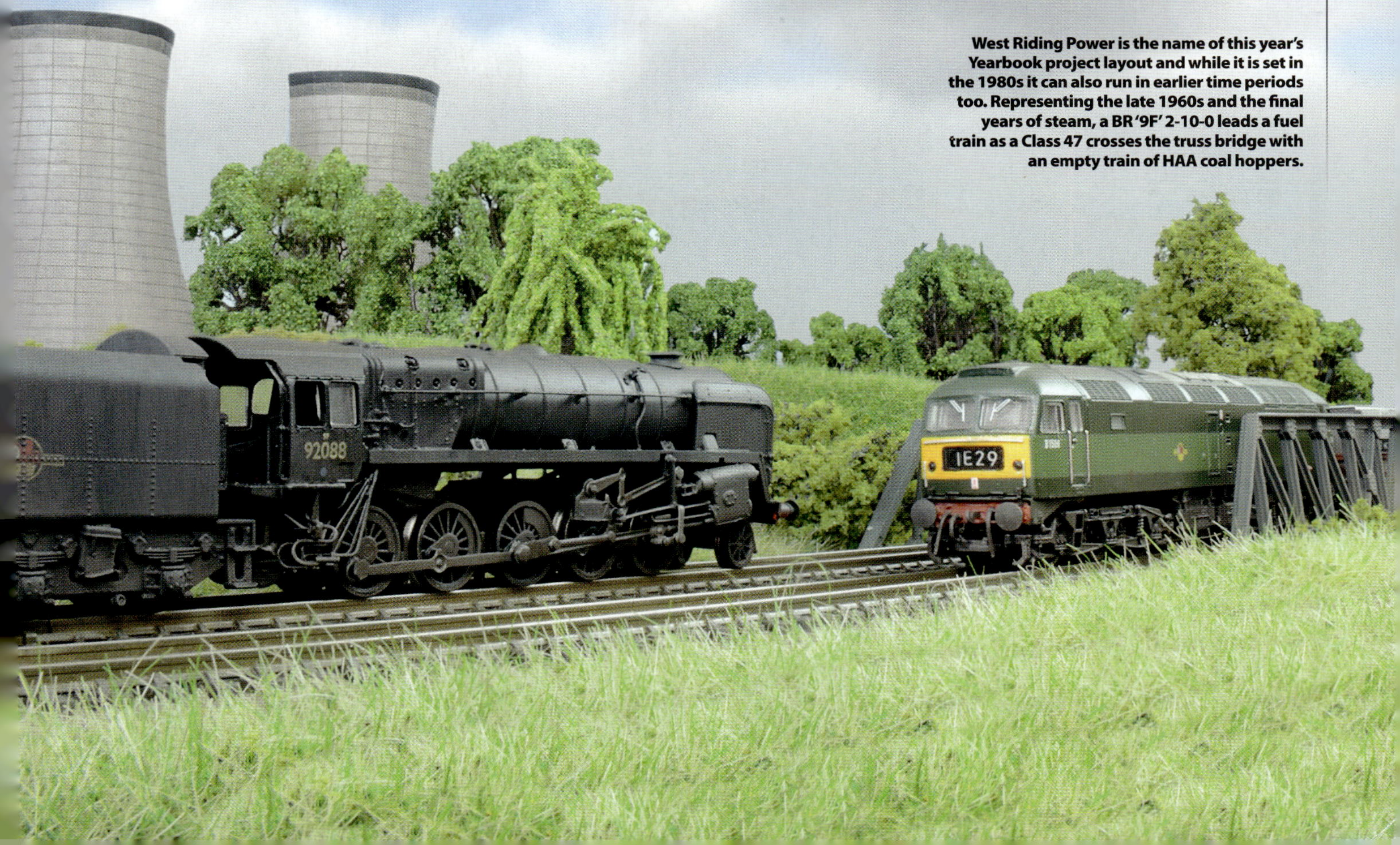

West Riding Power is the name of this year's Yearbook project layout and while it is set in the 1980s it can also run in earlier time periods too. Representing the late 1960s and the final years of steam, a BR '9F' 2-10-0 leads a fuel train as a Class 47 crosses the truss bridge with an empty train of HAA coal hoppers.

Introducing WEST RIDING POWER

Inspired by a new collection of buildings together with photographs from the 1980s **MIKE WILD** set out to build a new compact exhibition layout in 'N' gauge for *Hornby Magazine* with a power station as its focal feature.

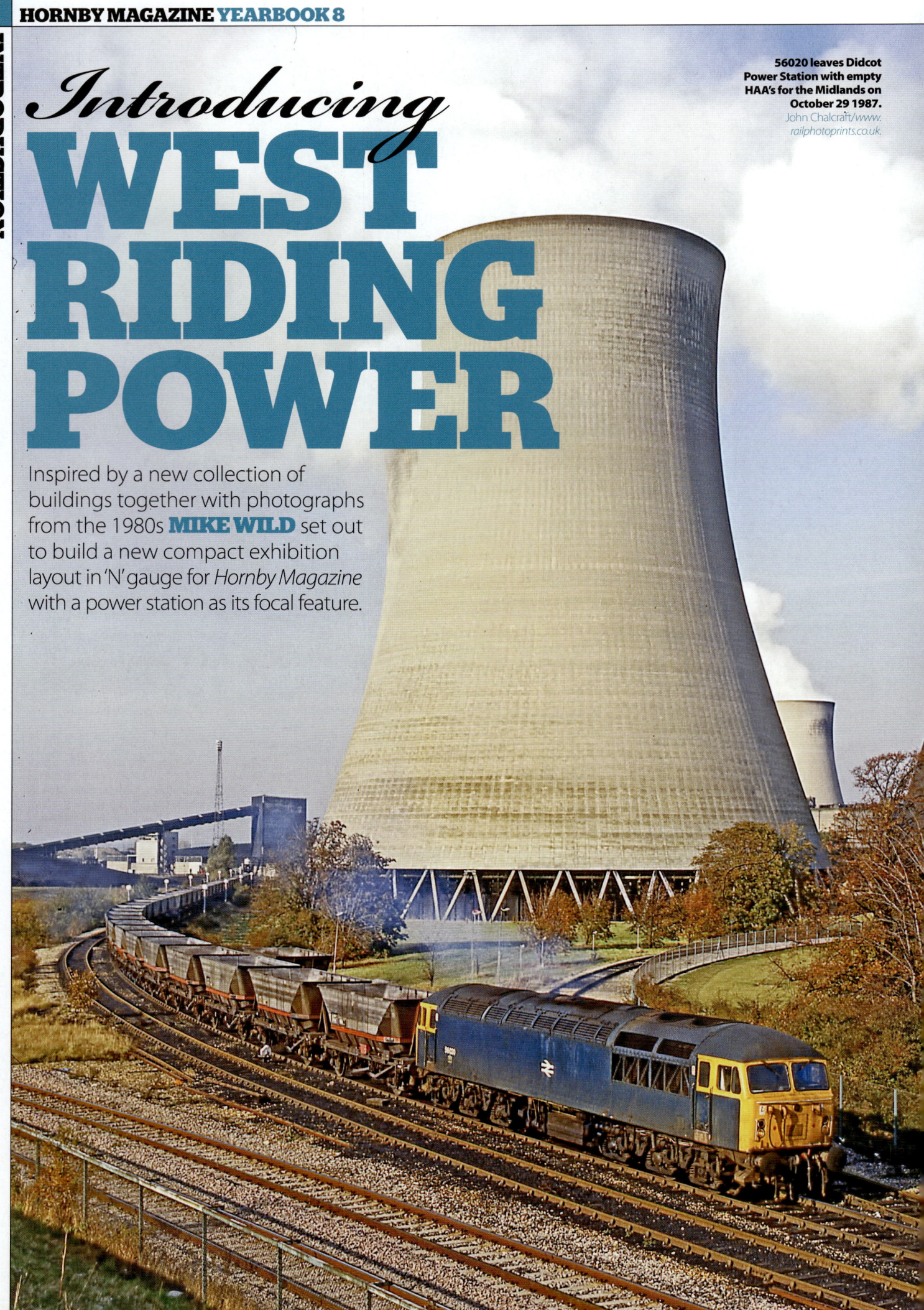

56020 leaves Didcot Power Station with empty HAA's for the Midlands on October 29 1987. *John Chalcraft/www.railphotoprints.co.uk.*

On the model we wanted to create a sense of distance between the main line and the power station circuit. This mock up showed how things might look with a river bridge in the foreground.

TOOLS FOR BASEBOARD CONSTRUCTION
» Handsaw
» Pencil
» Tape measure
» Tri-square
» Electric screwdriver

SOMETIMES LAYOUT IDEAS just spring up before our eyes. We'd been planning something totally different for this year's *Hornby Magazine Yearbook*, but when the opportunity to create a model of a power station came our way it was hard to refuse.

Having spent many hours driving up and down the A1 and across the M62 the sight of cooling towers has been common for me. Those at Ferrybridge where the two trunk roads meet together with West Burton Power station near Gainsborough are the ones I've seen the most. The giant proportions of their facilities and the knowledge that trainloads of coal, at least at one time, served these giant electricity generators have always drawn interest and I well remember seeing trainloads of coal in HAA Merry Go Round hoppers running at places like Chesterfield, York, Barnetby (although admittedly for Scunthorpe steelworks use)

and many other locations which were equally impressive.

The face of coal traffic has changed dramatically over the years, but it has always been a major part of railway operations. In the pre-grouping and pre-nationalisation era it was wooden bodied four-wheel open wagons which transported the black mineral while in BR steam days the influx of steel bodied mineral wagons in 16ton and 21ton formats took over. 20ton hoppers were introduced in the 1950s as well.

However, in the mid-1960s a brand new wagon design arrived in the HAA merry-go-round hopper and more recently high capacity bogie wagons have been used for the transport of coal.

With all that and a desire to build a BR blue period layout the die was cast for a project which would feature a different period from anything that we had built before but, as I will explain, a layout that can also be run in a variety of eras in the future too.

Power stations

The first power station in England featuring water powered dynamos was built in Northumberland in the 1860s and this led on to steam powered power stations within 20 years. Widespread introduction of large power stations began in the 1920s with some, including Battersea in London, receiving coal deliveries by water. Ferrybridge A power station – built in 1926-1927 - was connected directly to the London and North Eastern Railway (LNER) for delivery of coal while the smaller station at Hartshead in North West England was also supplied by rail. The latter had sidings which could hold 130 12ton wagons which were discharged into a hopper underneath the sidings for movement to the power station via a conveyor belt system.

As demands for power increased so did the requirement for coal as the fuel for power stations, leading to increased use of rail transport. Following formation of the Central »

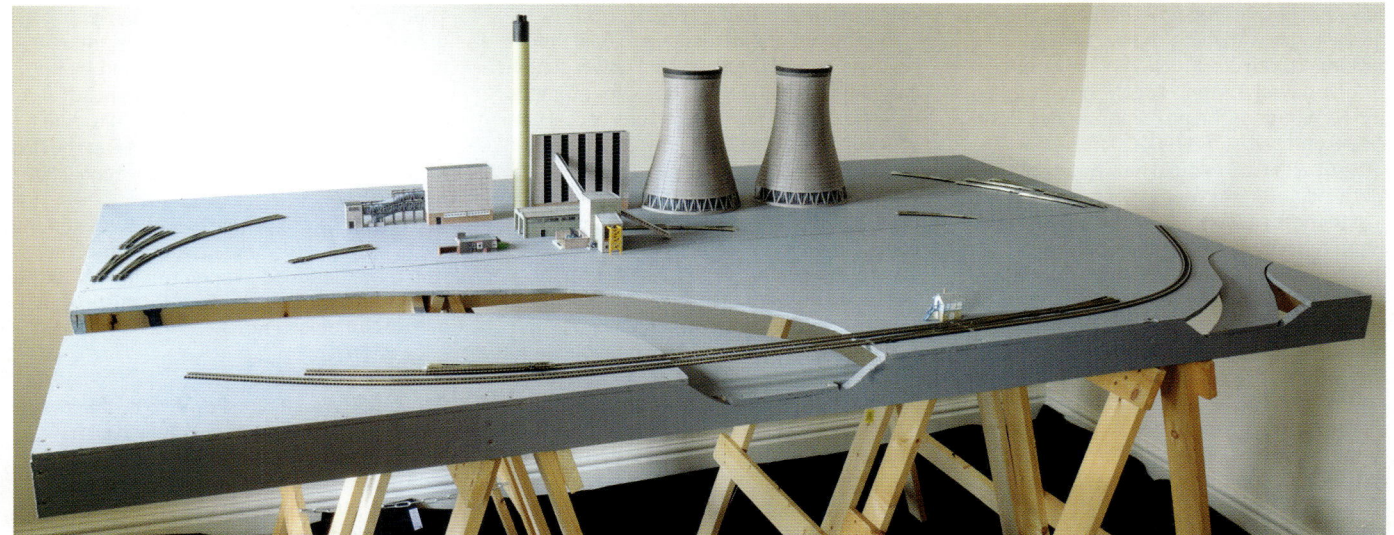

Having built the baseboard using 9mm plywood for the surface and 69mm x 18mm timber for the frame we had a base to work from. Painting the surface provides a smart and clean working area.

Mocking up the buildings from the Bachmann Scenecraft collection showed just how much space we really needed to make this model work. The final footprint chosen is 6ft 6in x 4ft.

Electricity Generating Board (CEGB) in 1957 a new form of coal fired power station – the ones we see today with giant cooling towers – was developed with construction of new plants including West Burton, Didcot, Eggborough and Ferrybridge C being commissioned during the second half of the 1960s.

The CEGB's plan to build new power stations saw a change in the method of delivery of coal to these sites and BR developed the HAA 33ton capacity four-wheel hopper wagon. These new wagons were designed to speed up the process of coal deliveries and replaced thousands of four-wheel open wagons of the 16ton and 21ton mineral designs. Other sites were designed from the outset to operate with earlier 20ton hoppers.

West Burton power station was used to test the new wagons which could be unloaded on the move combined with new slow speed control equipment for locomotives which meant the aptly named Merry Go Round (MGR) trains technically never had to stop moving. Cockenzie power station in Scotland was the first to receive trainloads of HAA hoppers for coal deliveries in 1966.

The amount of coal required to fulfil the requirements of these modern power stations was phenomenal. Ferrybridge C for example initially required four million tons of coal per year which meant 17 1,000ton trains were required every day!

Motive power selected for MGR trains was initially Class 47s but later the slow speed control equipment was also fitted to Class 20s which operated in pairs. Classes 56, 58, 59, 60 and 66 were all fitted with slow speed control gear during construction for use on such trains. The change to the more powerful Type 5 diesels such as the '56' and '58' brought an increase in train lengths too to around 35 wagons.

Building a model of a power station calls for compromise – even in 'N' gauge – as the sites occupied by these facilities are gigantic. They have an interesting mix of ground cover too ranging from neatly kept fresh green grass to black mountains of coal and sleek concrete structures with tarmac roads in between. The size of the plant depended upon its output with some plants featuring eight or more cooling towers and multiple turbines. For example the 26 acre site at Hartshead developed 64 megawatts while the 410 acre site at West Burton A power station was the first to be built with a capability of delivering 2,000 megawatts.

To deliver coal to power 1960s power stations the railway typically threads around the site with those designed to operate with HAA MGR hoppers having balloon loops for the operation of trains for unloading.

Period choice

We wanted West Riding Power to be different from our previous layouts – all of which have represented the BR steam and transition era through the 1950s and 1960s. This layout is primarily set in the 1980s to offer something completely different but still allow for a wide variety of locomotives and rolling stock.

The 1980s were an interesting time. Plain

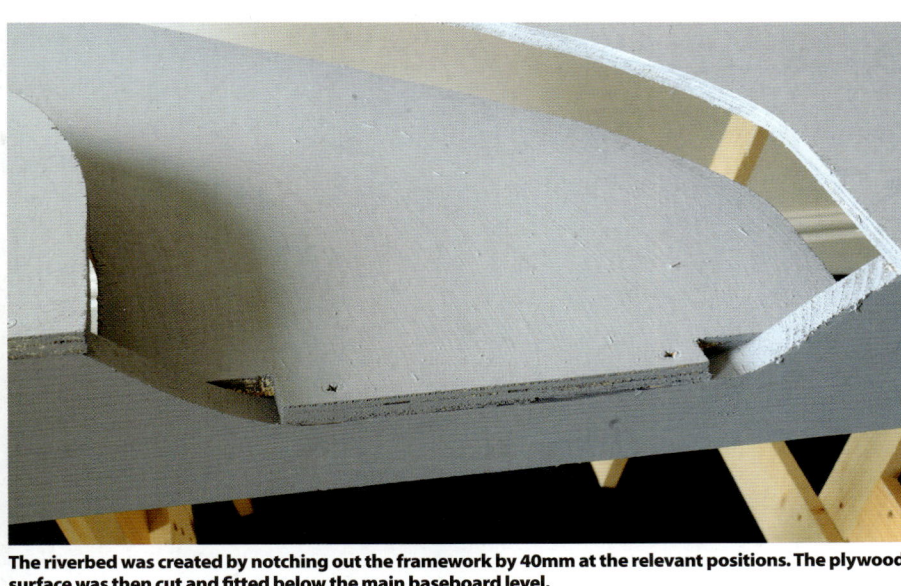

The riverbed was created by notching out the framework by 40mm at the relevant positions. The plywood surface was then cut and fitted below the main baseboard level.

corporate blue was giving way to the influx of 'large logo' blue and Railfreight grey with red solebar stripes which brought a fresh new look to locomotives and rolling stock. It was still a railway bound by the steam age though and vacuum braked wagons were an everyday sight alongside new air braked vehicles and those which had been converted with through piping.

Our research has shown up some fascinating train formations which we intend to model and has also shown that while BR had made the most of its new HAA coal hoppers, the 16ton and 21ton mineral wagons and 20ton hoppers were far from extinct on coal flows. As such we have the opportunity to run trains of all types if we wish.

However, we also wanted to create a layout with flexibility to its period and while the 1980s is our primary target it can also be run as a late 1960s – circa 1968-1970 – or in the sectorisation or privatisation periods, assuming we have enough rolling stock. The 1968-1970 time period is interesting too as it allows us to represent the last year of steam traction with '9F' 2-10-0s, '8F' 2-8-0s and 'Black Five' 4-6-0s running alongside diesel locomotives in two tone green, plain green and BR blue and hauling a variety of stock. With MGR hopper trains starting in 1965 alongside the Central Electricity Generating Board's investment in new power stations it gives the chance to represent a different period in railway history which is gaining popularity.

Moving forwards the layout can easily be run in the 1990s period too covering sectorisation and the early moves towards privatisation of freight operations with the introduction of Loadhaul, Mainline and Transrail liveries. This would also see a complete change in passenger trains as the early 1980s period still calls for locomotive hauled workings while, in the West Riding at least, the vast majority of longer distance passenger work was turned over to Diesel Multiple Units (DMUs) from the late 1980s with the introduction of Class 150, 156 and 158 units.

The final time period on our potential list is the first decade of the 21st century when a raft of new liveries came into being and new locomotives, such as the Class 66 and 67 diesels, could be seen operating side by side with older designs and in a mixture of liveries.

All this means that West Riding Power has a great deal of potential to keep us entertained putting together stock for different periods, but for now the 1980s will be the main focus of the project.

Planning

The aim of the layout is to represent a double track main line running around the outside with a secondary circuit off the main line to reach the power station. Developing a model of a power station within the confines of a relatively small footprint provides a number of challenges.

The first step was to acquire a sheet of plywood and begin mocking up the trackplan we had in mind. Adding in the buildings, a rake of HAA hoppers and a set of seven Mk 1 carriages helped to create a clear picture of what we would be working with and how much space it would need to accommodate everything.

The total space available for the project was originally set at 5ft x 4ft, but this soon proved too small once the buildings were laid out and it would also have restricted the length of trains too – the target being for a minimum of 15 wagons in an MGR formation, roughly half of what would be expected in the real world behind Class 56 and 58 diesels.

Having established this we decided on a final footprint of 6ft 6in x 4ft which allows space to accommodate a seven coach High Speed Train (HST) in one of the storage yard lines as well as ample scope to model HAA train formations of up to 16 wagons.

The largest compromise comes in the arrangement of the track through the unloading building. At full size power stations balloon loops were built where the train would loop back on itself and leave the site where it entered. In model form this would have required our layout footprint to be bigger still and pushing somewhere in the region of 8ft x 5ft to do it justice. This, for our purposes, was too much so an alternative trackplan was needed.

The final plan sees a single track loop leave the inner main line, run through the unloading shed and return to join the inner main line at the opposite end of the layout creating a secondary circuit within the main double track main line. This means that departing trains continue in the same direction as that which they arrived – our fictional story being that »

WHAT WE USED – THE BUILDINGS	
BUILDINGS	**CAT NO.**
Rail interchange shed	42-196
Coal distribution building	42-197
Power station chimney	42-198
Low relief cooling tower	42-297
Low relief boiler house	42-298
Low relief turbine hall	42-299
Bicycle hut	42-140
Shunters mess room	42-139

WHAT WE USED – THE BASEBOARD
- 9mm plywood – 8ft x 4ft sheet cut to size at DIY store
- 69mm x 18mm planed softwood
- 4.0 x 30mm twin thread wood screws
- Grey emulsion paint

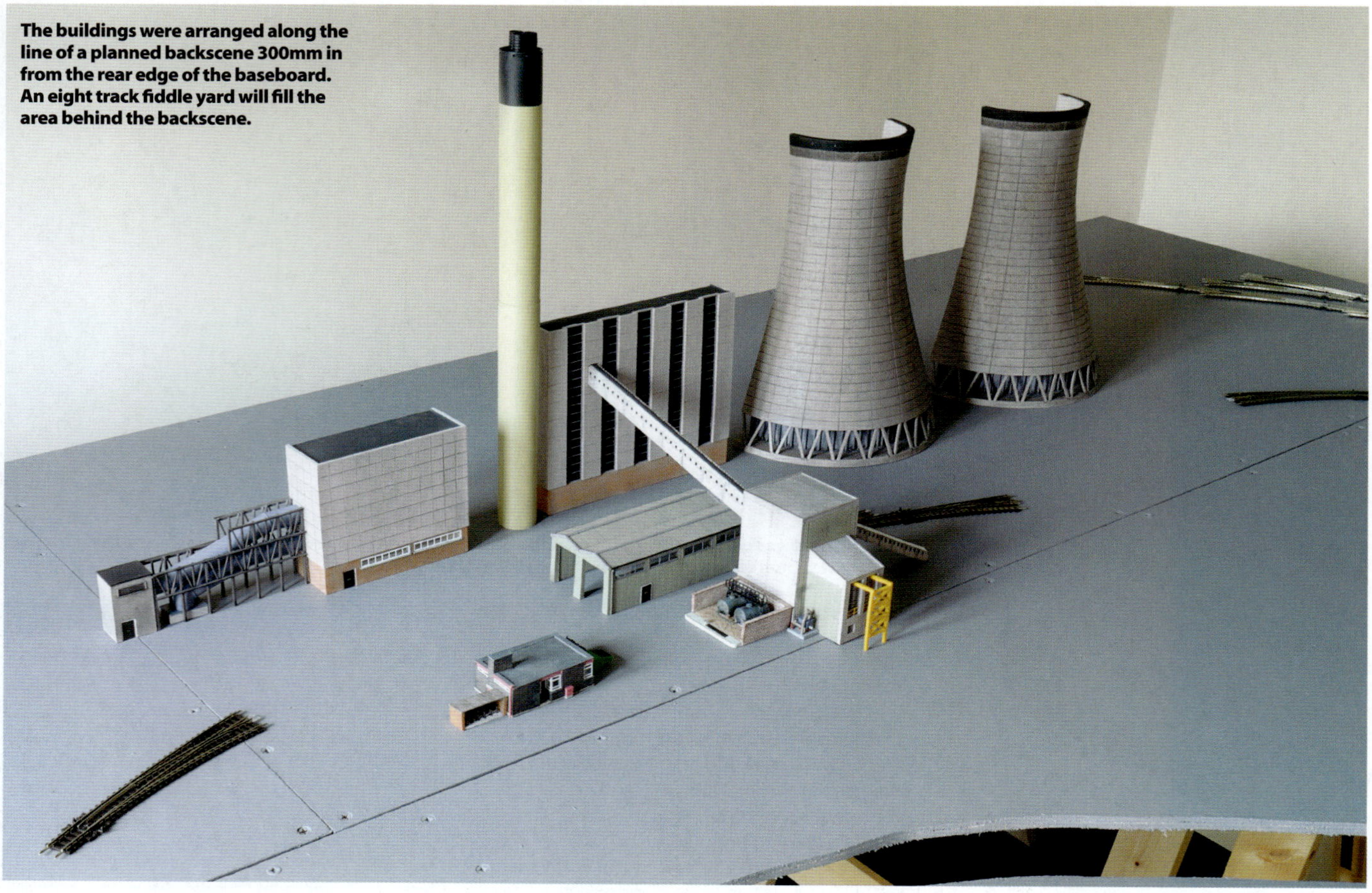

The buildings were arranged along the line of a planned backscene 300mm in from the rear edge of the baseboard. An eight track fiddle yard will fill the area behind the backscene.

the location of this power station leads to a junction further up the line to turn the trains back towards the colliery for reloading. In practice this all works well and the trains 'look' right in model terms as they round the sharp curves to the power station area.

The main lines are very straightforward and consists simply of a pair of tracks making a complete circuit of the baseboard. The only other pointwork on the main lines is a crossover adjacent to the entry to the power station loop. At the rear of the layout hidden behind the backscene is an eight track fiddle yard which offers scope for up to 14 trains to be accommodated depending on their length. Reaching this level does require multiple trains to be 'stacked' in some loops but ultimately this offers increased variety for operation.

The temptation with this type of layout would be to build a solid top flat baseboard as that suits the purpose of a power station model well. However, another feature which we associated with power stations is water so we decided that it would help break up the layout if a waterway was built into the front of the two baseboards passing beneath the main line in two places. Added to this we decided on a road going down a hill in one corner below the level of the railway to increase the variation in height across the model.

Building the baseboard

Two baseboards make up the foundations for West Riding Power. Both are identical in size and measure 6ft 6in x 2ft to allow enough room for all the trimmings of the model as well as appropriate train lengths for the fiddle yard.

The boards are made with 9mm plywood for the tops with 69mm x 18mm softwood timber for the frames. This was all cut to length and fixed to the baseboard top with 4.0 x 30mm woodscrews with cross-members in between to create a strong and rigid baseboard.

The front scenic board was slightly more complex with the introduction of the riverbed and roadway to take care of. Rather than opting for a traditional open frame baseboard we used the depth of the framework timbers to our advantage cutting 40mm deep notches to accommodate the riverbed on the front and left hand edges together with a third notch at the right hand end for the road to drop down to. The surface was then cut to suit the available spaces and the whole assembled using the same woodscrews as the rear solid top board.

Having built the board the whole assembly was painted grey to seal the timber and provide a clean surface on which to start laying track. It also avoids the natural colour of the plywood top showing through should any scenery be chipped or scratched in the future.

With the basics done, the bridges mocked up and the track ready to lay West Riding Power was ready to move forward from bare baseboard to a working railway as we explain in the next instalment on pages 44-51. ■

To add further variation in height a road way with a gradient was introduced in one corner of the baseboard.

WEST RIDING POWER TRACK DIAGRAM (Not to scale)

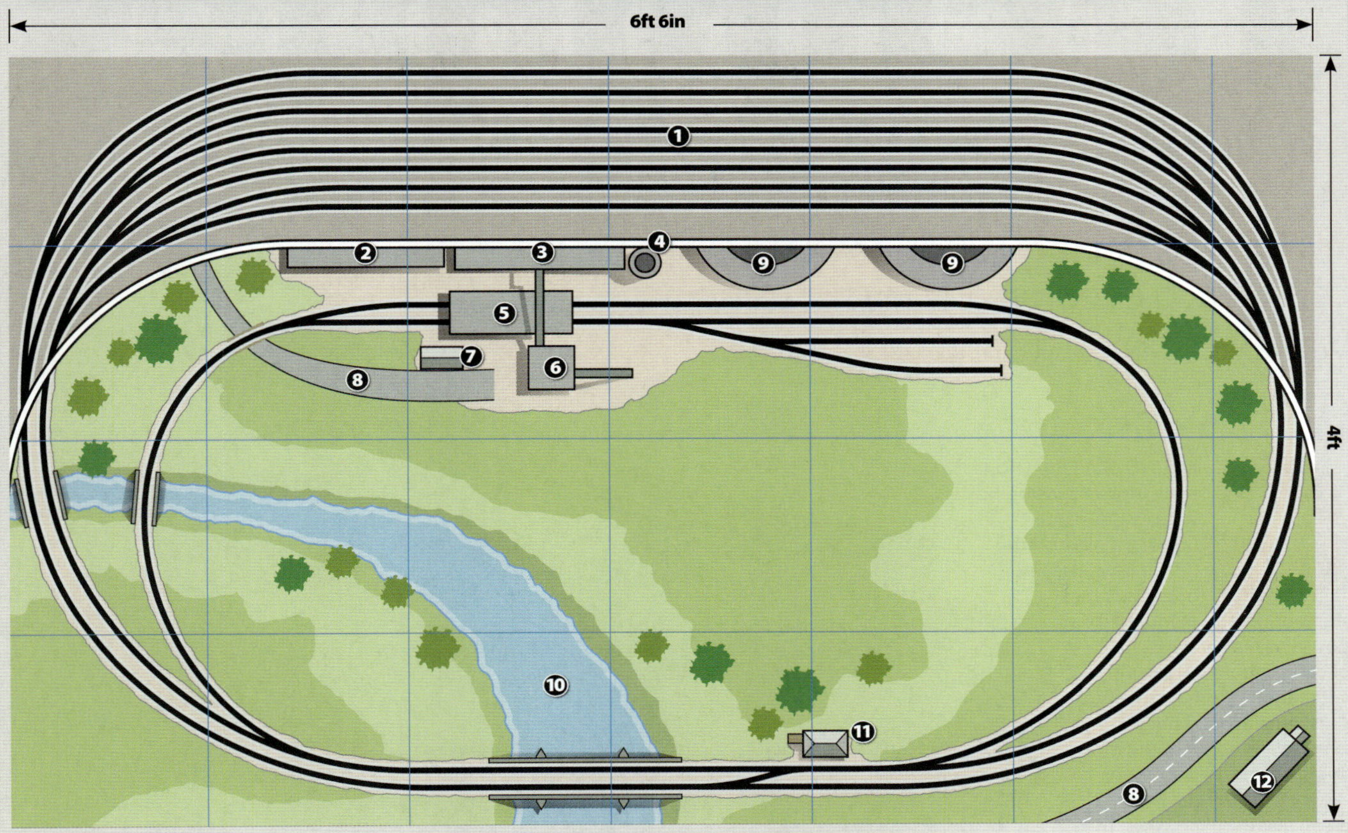

6ft 6in · 4ft

KEY
1. Storage yard
2. Turbine Hall
3. Boiler house
4. Chimney
5. Interchange shed
6. Distribution plant
7. Office
8. Road
9. Cooling tower
10. River
11. Disused signalbox
12. Church

Unloading of the HAA hoppers was done automatically on the move. 26005 inches through the discharge point at Cockenzie Power Station as it delivers another load of coal from the nearby Blindwells Opencast site (on the other side of the East Coast Main Line at Tranent), on August 13 1982. *John Chalcraft/www.railphotoprints.co.uk.*

Techniques

Covering the bare baseboards requires vegetation as well as structures. **NIGEL BURKIN** shows how easily it can be achieved on any layout using a variety of products and techniques.

GROUND COVER MODELLING consisting of grasses, bushes, scrub, weeds and flowering plants is the first of several layers of scenery that starts bringing a layout to life. Covering plaster hard shell or carved foam terrain with vegetation is some of the most satisfying layout work you will ever do and some of the most forgiving too.

But it isn't all about fresh green grasses and bushes. There is another side to ground cover and that is soil, earth, gravel and sand which may be exposed in dirt tracks, gravel roads, beaches along the course of rivers and where the plants have been eroded away. In fact almost anything you apply to the surface of your terrain could be called 'ground cover', including water, rail ballast, rocks, paved roads, garden modelling, trees and snow.

Before reaching for packets of turf and a bottle of scenery glue, take a look at some reference photographs to see how the landscape appears in your chosen area of modelling. Consider the time of the year in which your layout is set because colours change with the seasons and the same grasses, weeds and bushes will look different. Look at factors which affect the growth of ground cover including how livestock affects the growth of grasses in pasture compared to the less manicured environment of railway embankments. How do weeds and grasses grow in urban and industrial areas? What trees and plants are the first to populate brown field sites such as old railway yards? Photographs will help you with determining how much ground cover looks right.

Choosing ground cover 'vegetation'

Scenery materials have developed dramatically in recent times with the traditional dyed sawdust giving way to considerably more refined and better-coloured products for ground cover vegetation. Ground foam is now giving way to static grass which has seen its use grow in the last ten years particularly as the price of static grass applicators has fallen.

Scenery material suppliers such as Noch and Mininatur offer ground cover materials to represent specific features including cereal crops, meadow grasses, cattle and livestock pasture, rough ground and wild ground cover. The seasons are also taken into consideration with products coloured to suit, making ground cover modelling a satisfyingly precise area of landscape modelling in its own right.

Whatever lengths you plan to go to, the majority of experienced modellers choose to use static grass as the main component of green ground cover now, the idea is to achieve the correct colouring for your chosen season and a variety of textures. The real landscape has a variety of colours and textures which, when replicated on a layout, will make it appear more realistic.

For example, livestock will eat pasture grasses down, sometimes leaving the tougher broadleaf weeds alone. Bracken will grow pretty well unchecked in upland areas where acid soil dominates – it is rarely eaten by anything, being

GROUND COVER

Experimenting with a small diorama allows you to make mistakes and try new modelling materials before applying them to a layout where corrections may be harder to do. This diorama was built to test some dirt road ideas and to demonstrate basic ground cover techniques.

landscaping, but like any mechanically applied material, can appear too uniform in appearance. There are several ways of avoiding the artificial appearance and one simple method involves mixing different sizes of static grass in the applicator and applying them at the same time. Another technique is to drift a second layer of straw-coloured grass over the first in selected areas to vary the height of the grasses. Push some over to flatten the grass in one or two areas. Add a smattering of ground foam material in places to represent weeds, particularly in areas where hedging and bushes will be planted. Choose darker colours to represent broadleaf weeds and wild flowers. Remember: texture and colour is important when selecting 'green' ground cover materials and always choose those advertised as colour-fast.

Hardstanding

Not all ground cover consists of vegetation and not all ground is covered by grasses and weeds. Dirt tracks and roads together with hardstanding and areas of bare ground are just as important features to model. On the practice diorama featured in this article, the semi-abandoned industrial scene features areas of hardstanding and little used dirt road.

Areas of bare soil, tracks and dirt roads are not easy to create convincingly and some modellers go to extraordinary lengths to achieve an acceptable result. A simple technique involves the use of earth coloured acrylic paint or powder paint mixed with water and a quantity of fine sand. The use of fast-drying PVA glue is the key ingredient, binding the sand together in the road surface. It is brushed on and various markings can be introduced into it to represent ploughing, tyre tracks and other features. Colouring can be dark for industrial areas and dark or peaty soils. Choose lighter colouring for dry sandy soils and dry gravel tracks. Remember that water will make gravel, sand and soil appear darker.

Other options include the use of landscaping plaster for creating dirt roads and areas of bare earth. Woodland Scenics Hydrocal plaster is easily dyed with pigments and acrylic paints to achieve a good colour before it is applied to the layout. Air drying clays are also popular materials for making effective dirt tracks and roads, being soft enough to introduce tyre tracks and ruts. Once hardened, they may be painted and treated »

relatively toxic to livestock and will grow to the exclusion of other plants. Lineside locations such as embankments and cuttings will see longer grasses and bushes growing together with weeds. All of these features have their own textures and cannot be created with just one or two applications of ground cover material.

Colour is another factor to consider. I prefer late Summer as a modelling season as grasses and weeds reach their maximum height. Whilst the underlying colour of grass will be green, the longer strands and flower stalks will likely be dry and straw-coloured. Winter grasses will be dead and dried to a straw colour, together with what is left of Summer weeds which may be dark brown. Not all grasses stand tall – they can be beaten down by rain and wind and early summer grasses will be a lovely fresh green but not very tall. Areas of good drainage will result in prematurely dry grasses, such as the area immediately adjacent to the permanent way and dirt roads. Creating these textures is the route to making your landscape modelling appear convincing.

Static grass has done much for realistic

GROUND COVER TECHNIQUES

1 A cursory search on the internet will reveal a wide variety of scenery products suitable for mass ground cover including ground foam of various textures and static grasses in various lengths.

2 Javis offers a variety of scatter materials in its scenery range which are at the lower cost end of the market. They hark back to the days of dyed sawdust and whilst they have value in ground cover modelling, they are most effective as accents rather than mass ground cover.

3 Woodland Scenics offers a variety of ground foam products in fine and coarse grades. They are very useful for first layers, accents and in some cases, larger areas of ground cover vegetation.

4 The Model Tree Shop has a very useful range of ground foam scenery products together with static grasses ideal for ground cover scenery – not to mention trees.

with a little fine sand to make them appear dusty and gravelly.

Where there are tracks, bare ground and dirt roads, there will be weeds and grasses – they will not be entirely barren. Clumps of weeds can be represented with pieces of ground foam and grass tufts applied. Short grasses may grow in a strip along the hump between the tyre tracks. Usually, the colour of such grasses is lighter than those found on railway embankments and cuttings.

Making the difference
There is scope to give your ground cover some individuality by adding some scenery accents. Grass tufts can be home-made with a static grass applicator and applied to tracks, the edges of structures and along the bottom of walls. Weeds are introduced with a smattering of coarse ground foam as long as it is a slightly different shade of green – usually darker. Again, the choice of such accents and colouring will depend on the season. Wild flowers are unlikely to be found in late Autumn or Winter yet make a lovely accent when applied to the smattering of ground foam used to add further weedy texture to static grass.

A different way of making grass clumps is to use separate grass fibres such as the field grass range by Woodland Scenics or the long bundles of dyed fibre by Anitor Décor. They are cut to length and planted using a spot of scenery glue. A tiny amount of fine ground foam is applied to the base of the clump to disguise the glue used to secure them.

It is important not to go overboard with accents in your ground cover. Many areas of the layout treated with ground cover vegetation should remain neutral so as not to detract from layout scenes and cameos. Nonetheless, a little interest can be added, depending on the season being modelled, by adding flowers (Woodland Scenics flowering foliage is ideal for this), specific plants representing weeds together with rocks and plant debris such as old tree branches and stumps. It is worth looking at the Noch range of laser cut plants for accents which would suit a particular scene.

Alternative materials
There are plenty of options for scenic materials. For a long time sticking down medical lint bandage and leaving it to dry before ripping the backing away to leave the texture of long grass was popular. This was dyed or painted different colours with accents applied. Faux fur is growing in popularity for the same reason.

Some modellers are attracted to the natural colours of hanging basket liner, although my experiments showed that it can be both inconsistent from one packet to the next and is not colour fast. The texture of hanging basket liner is perfect for the modelling of scrub and long grasses in wild areas of the layout. The colour can be supplemented with the use of dilute acrylic paints.

Good old fashioned plumber's hemp makes excellent grasses too and its natural colour is a close representation of dried grasses. It can be dyed a variety of shades of green and beige with »

The contrast between grazed sheep pasture and the longer grasses on the railway side of the fence is clearly seen in this July scene. The grasses are already long with dry upper leaves and seed heads. The grass in the pasture is greener but worn down to leave some exposed soil along sheep tracks.

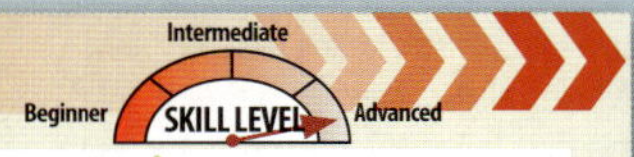

Static grasses are available in a variety of lengths and colours from the suppliers of scenery products. The grass shown in this photograph is 4.5mm long Late Fall by MiniNatur. Other manufacturers include Noch, Woodland Scenics and Javis.

A small diorama is the perfect way to develop ground cover techniques and test colours before applying them to a large project layout. The scene will feature an area of rough ground with long grasses and weeds.

10 TIPS
Successful ground cover vegetation

1. Choose adhesives carefully – they must dry clear and matt

2. Materials used for ground cover must be colour-fast

3. Use photographs as reference for seasonal colour and size of plants

4. Avoid uniformity of ground cover and use accents to bring it to life

5. Always paint plaster hard shell or foam terrain with a good coat of brown or green paint before applying ground cover.

6. Ground cover includes the modelling of dirt roads, bare earth and tracks which should be completed before adding 'green' scenery.

7. Apply static grass to a thin layer of fine ground foam cover and use more than one size of fibre for variety.

8. Look for alternative materials which will add texture and interest to the landscape including plumbers' hemp (which has to be dyed) and hanging basket liner (if it is the right colour).

9. Apply the same materials consistently over the layout for a neat finish and keep notes of successful techniques and the materials used.

10. Ground cover materials can be used to blend in specific features to make them look part of the landscape.

clothing dyes to suit a particular season and cut to a variety of lengths with sharp scissors. Along similar lines, hemp rope and string is a useful material together with postiche as used to make theatrical wigs. Whatever you plan to use, be sure you can acquire it throughout the layout project.

Finally, commercial grass mats deserve a mention. Although they are sometimes regarded as being in the sphere of tabletop train sets; some modellers will cut them into specific shapes to suit areas of open ground. Accents, bushes and other vegetation are added, especially along the edges of the mat to blend them in, to break up the uniform appearance of the mat.

Suitable adhesives

Choosing the right adhesives is important because the last thing you want is your carefully applied scenery material coming adrift during handling and transport of the layout! The various manufacturers of scenery products and modelling chemicals offer a variety of specific adhesives including scatter glues, dedicated glue for static grass and general scenic cements. Products such as Deluxe Materials Scatter Grip are very useful for applying the first layer of 'scatter' on the landscape. Woodland Scenics Scenic Cement is used in a variety of ways and may be applied using a spray bottle or a brush.

Firm-hold non-perfumed hairspray is the perfect spray adhesive for touching up tree foliage and for adding further layers of static grass. Cheap and easy to use, it is applied in small amounts and in a well ventilated space! Avoid over-application because its sticky consistency can leave visible traces which will appear shiny!

The choice of adhesive is a very personal one. I used just two adhesives to complete the ground cover treatment in the diorama here. The first was simple fast drying PVA glue which was used neat and diluted with water to varying degrees to suit the application. The other material was Scenic Cement by Woodland Scenics which is also fast drying. In both cases, the adhesives dry matt and clear, leaving no trace residue on the layout. For once, I avoided hairspray! ■

GROUND COVER TECHNIQUES

7 The underlying topography consists of plaster hard shell on a cardboard lattice frame to keep the project simple. Some small scenic details and a length of track are positioned on the diorama to gauge how it will look.

8 Ground cover application commenced by coating the white plaster hard shell with a water-based earth-coloured paint.

9 The track is coloured and various scenic features added including the board crossing and loading bank. The storage container will be permanently added to the scene once ground cover is complete.

10 Dirt roads and areas of exposed earth or soil are ground cover and are the next areas to be added to the diorama using a mix of paint, PVA glue and fine sand for texture.

11 The colour of dirt roads and hardstanding is built up using different mud and soil coloured paints or specific products such as MIG earth and soil pigments.

12 Pigments and water based paints used to build up the road and bare soil colours can be applied with craft brushes. Don't spoil your expensive sable paint brushes on scenery work!

BUILDING A PRACTICE PIECE

Building a small practice diorama is always a useful exercise. Experienced modellers use them to develop techniques and to try new materials before applying them to the layout. I wanted to experiment with dirt roads and hardstanding techniques for a particular project and constructed a simple diorama with the aim of testing some different pigments for industrial dirt roads. As it happens, it also needed some general ground cover vegetation too!

GROUND COVER

Ground cover is at its most effective when it is built up in layers with each new layer adding depth and texture. This is *Hornby Magazine's* office test track, Topley Dale, which was built for Yearbook No. 5 with a Hornby Peppercorn 'K1' 2-6-0 crossing the viaduct.

13 Ground cover vegetation follows on from the dirt and soil cover. A good layer of PVA glue diluted with water to the consistency of dairy cream so it would not run down the slope was applied to the painted hard shell.

14 Fine turf is applied to the glue layer, dispensed from a plastic cup rather than the bag.

15 The turf layer is sprayed with Scenic Cement using a recycled hand pumped sprayer to ensure it is completely glued in place. A second sprayed application of Scenic Cement prepares the area for static grass.

16 The first coat of grass is applied using an electric Noch applicator. Noch also offers an economical static grass bottle for working with small areas where the investment in an electric applicator cannot be justified.

GROUND COVER TECHNIQUES

Ground cover can also include some small bushes and scrub composed of anything from offcuts of sea foam trees, poly fibre, tree foliage and rubberised horsehair coated with foliage material. It can be used to blend in structures such as the loading bank to hide the gap between the wall and the hard shell surface.

The uniform application of static grass has been leavened with some weeds composed of ground foam and a shot of a different colour of grass. The glue mix was still wet when this picture was taken.

Another March scene, this time North of Stafford. The Freightliner Class 86s pass embankments with short grasses and weeds just beginning to grow after Winter. There are some long grass stems left over from the previous year – heavy rain and snow will normally beat them down. Dramatic low-angle photographs such as this one taken at the boundary fence are not possible at this location after May because the grasses grow too tall for a clear shot.

Intermediate
Beginner SKILL LEVEL Advanced

19

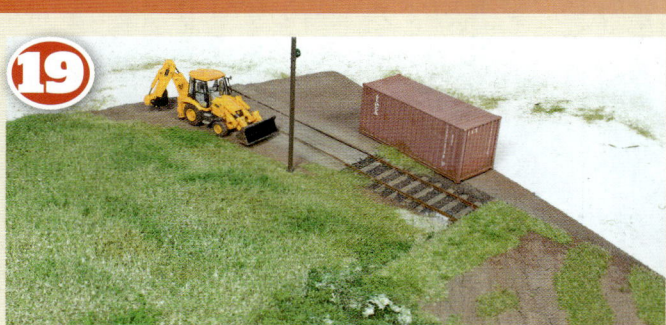

The worn dirt track on the loading bank has been treated with a smattering of different coloured 2mm long static grass whilst the main ground cover was given a final application of glue from the spray bottle to be sure it is well secured. Don't worry if the glue sits in the grasses for a while – it soon dries and disappears to leave a matt finish.

PRODUCT VARIETY

This article can only touch upon the vast range of ground cover materials suitable for popular modelling scales. A little time browsing the internet will turn up everything from clover pasture to hay, straw or summer grasses. The following web sites are a good place to start.

Noch	*www.noch.com*
Woodland Scenics	*www.bachmann.co.uk*
MiniNatur	*www.mininatur.de*
The Model Tree Shop	*www.themodeltreeshop.co.uk*
Hornby	*www.hornby.com*
Geoscenics	*www.geoscenics.co.uk*
Microscale	*www.jttmicroscale.com*
Gaugemaster	*www.gaugemaster.com*
Deluxe Materials	*www.deluxematerials.com*

20

Some cast plaster rocks have appeared on the diorama, together with scenic accents. The container has now been secured in place and will be blended in with grass tufts.

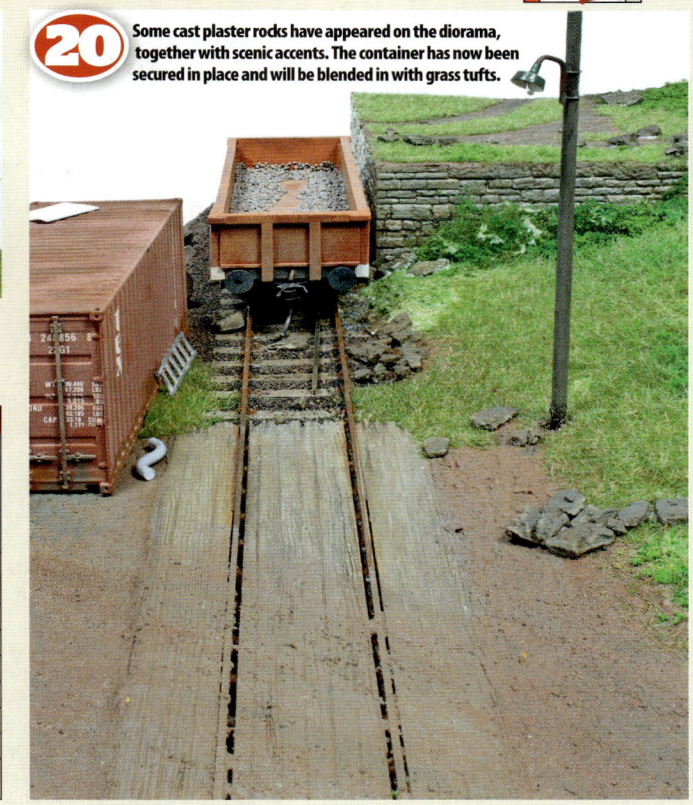

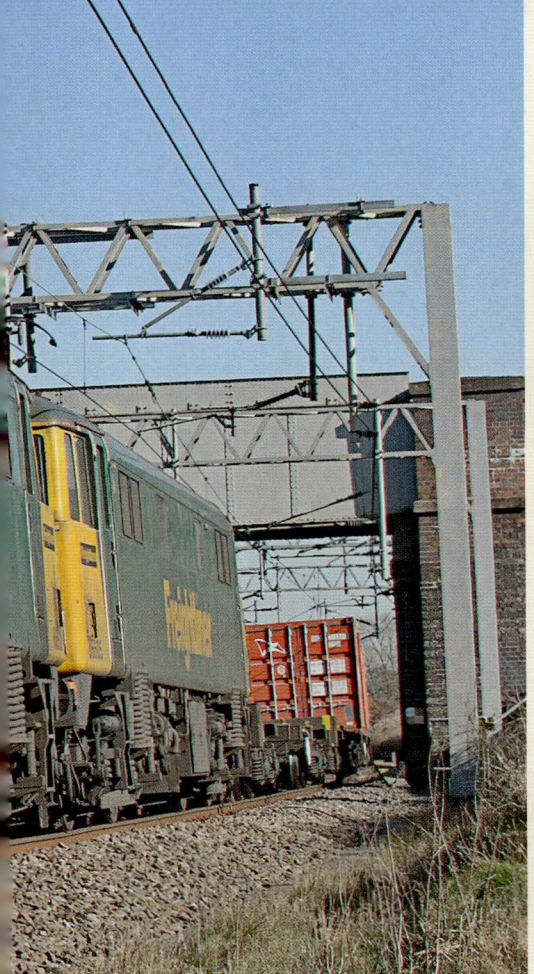

21

Whilst simple in appearance, the scene has allowed me to test some dirt road modelling techniques as well as having a little fun with some odds and ends from my scrap box! The scene now needs some scenic accents such as grass tufts to blend in features such as the solitary lamp post.

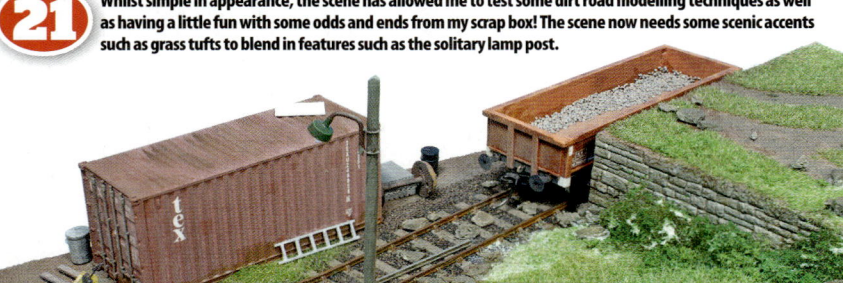

22

From white plaster hard shell to completed basic scenery – a few hours' work with simple scenery products and some earth paints has completely transformed the diorama.

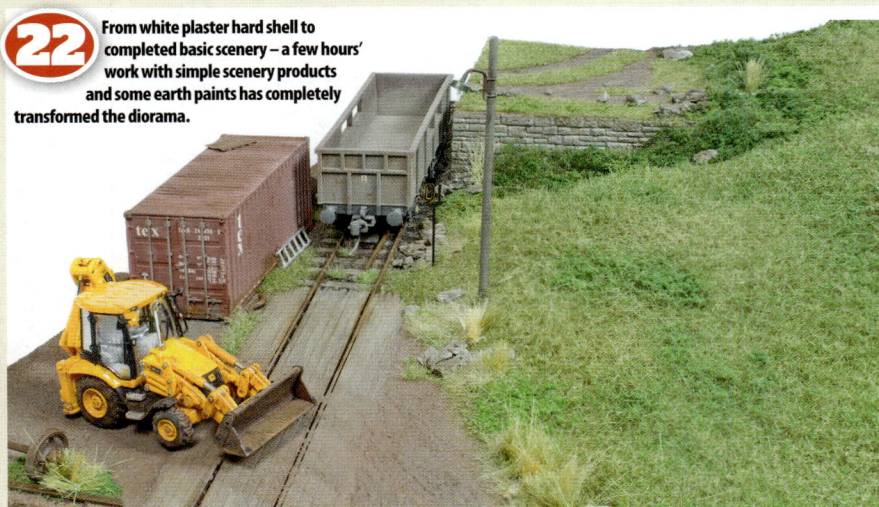

REALITY CHECK

Development of the British 4-6-0

One of the most successful and widely used configurations for British steam locomotives was the 4-6-0. This type underwent considerable development before becoming almost universal in the 1930s, as **EVAN GREEN-HUGHES** finds out.

ASK ANYONE brought up in the final years of steam which engines they remember best and almost certainly they will include a 4-6-0 in their list. The Western Region had its named 'Castles', 'Kings', 'Manors' and 'Halls'; the London Midland its 'Black Fives', 'Jubilees', 'Royal Scots' and 'Patriots'; the London and North Eastern had their 'B1s', 'Footballers' and 'B12s' while the Southern had its 'Lord Nelsons', 'H15s' and 'N15s'. Most of these were simply designed workaday locomotives with two outside cylinders built for general duties but others, particularly those from the Great Western Railway (GWR), were equipped with three or four cylinders and were used for the fastest and heaviest trains.

The type reached its zenith in the late 1930s and 1940s when hundreds of mixed traffic engines were being turned out and British Railways continued the tradition with its range of 'Standard' designs, which included two designs of 4-6-0s, the final ones of which were completed in 1957.

Fowler parallel boiler 'Royal Scot' 4-6-0 6168 *The Girl Guide* neasr Colwyn Bay with the Up 'Irish Mail' from Holyhead-Euston in 1938. These powerful three-cylinder engines were the LMS' answer to the GWR 'Castle' class. Rail Archive Stephenson.

The Highland Railway was the first to introduce 4-6-0s with delivery of the first 'Jones Goods' in 1894. 'Jones Goods' 4-6-0 17923 stands on the turntable at Inverness shed in May 1930. L.R. Tomsett/Rail Archive Stephenson.

American history

The origins of this highly-successful type go back to the mid 1800s in America where the 4-4-0 was the predominant wheel arrangement for more or less all forms of traffic. As the railway system in that country expanded lines were built into inhospitable terrain where there were more gradients while train weights increased due to the demands of a developing country.

The 4-4-0 was very successful but it suffered from a lack of adhesion due to much of its weight being carried on the front bogie wheels and its overall length limited the size of boiler that could be carried. One obvious answer was to increase the length of the locomotive by adding another powered axle. This alone increased the tractive effort due to more adhesive weight being available and was first done by the Philadelphia and Reading to spectacular effect - the resulting locomotives were copied by many other railroads. So successful did this wheel arrangement prove that the Americans coined the phrase the 'ten wheeler' to refer to such engines. »

HORNBY MAGAZINE YEARBOOK 8

REALITY CHECK

In Britain the requirements of the 19th century continued to be dealt with by the 4-4-0 but as larger engines were required many designers went for the simple expedient of adding a trailing axle to produce a 4-4-2. Engines of this wheel arrangement were often elegant and could be very fast but they were often prone to slipping which made them of limited use on heavy work or where the terrain was particularly hilly.

Scottish introduction

One area of the country which proved challenging to locomotive designers was the Highlands of Scotland where steep gradients and heavy freight trains required something more than the ubiquitous 0-6-0 that was then the almost universal haulier of goods trains. In 1894 the Locomotive Superintendent of the Highland Railway, David Jones, introduced Britain's first 4-6-0, the famous 'Jones Goods' class. These were at that time amongst the most powerful locomotives built in Britain and set out the principles of the 4-6-0s that were to follow over the next 60 years.

A large boiler was provided which worked at a pressure of 175psi, significantly higher than many other locomotives of the period, and this fed two outside cylinders of 20in bore and 26in stroke which were again larger than was usual at that time. Between September and November 1894 15 of these magnificent machines were constructed and they proved to be an outstanding success, often being used on passenger trains as well as for their intended goods work.

The Highland Railway went on to construct more 4-6-0s under Peter Drummond, this time for passenger work and these became known as the 'Castle' class while a third version designed by FG Smith and known as the 'River' class followed. These were notorious because when they began to be delivered the Highland Railway's civil engineer refused to accept them and they had to be sold to the Caledonian Railway, leading to Smith losing his job.

The North Eastern Railway (NER) was the first to introduce the 4-6-0 as a straight passenger engine with the first five being constructed at Gateshead to the design of Wilson Worsdell in 1899. These were intended to eliminate double-heading on heavy expresses between Newcastle and Edinburgh but were not a complete success. One reason for this was that they had been equipped with 6ft 1in driving wheels to cope with the gradients north of Berwick and consequently when running fast the mechanical parts were subject to overheating.

Two years later another batch of five was built to the same design but these were fitted with 6ft 8in diameter driving wheels and proved fast runners but too highly geared for climbing. When these engines were only a few months old Worsdell joined a management tour of the USA and was so impressed with the work being done by the 4-4-0s there that the idea of further development of 4-6-0s was abandoned. Despite this the original five 4-6-0s 2001-2010 were ideal traction for express goods trains and therefore a further 30 to this design were built between 1906 and 1909. The NER, having seemingly discovered by accident that the 4-6-0 was an ideal general purpose machine, went on to build a further batch of engines in 1911, these being fitted with 5ft 6in boilers and designated the 'S2'. All the NER locomotives can be readily identified by their being fitted with a very large cab with two side windows and enormous splashers.

Express freight

Over at the Great Central Railway (GCR) the adoption of the 4-6-0 was driven by the need to

The Great Western Railway's ultimate development of the 4-6-0 was its fleet of 30 'King' 4-6-0s. In 1946 6011 *King James I* **approaches Gerrards Cross station with the 6.10pm Paddington-Birkenhead Woodside express.**
C.R.L. Coles/Rail Archive Stephenson.

The fine lines of Peter Drummond's Highland Railway 'Castle' are captured by 140 *Taymouth Castle* on the turntable inside Inverness roundhouse in 1902. Rail Archive Stephenson.

work heavy trains of fish at express speeds from the east coast ports to London. Chief Engineer JG Robinson turned out his first 4-6-0 in 1902, this being fitted with driving wheels of only 6ft in diameter and becoming known, not surprisingly, as the 'fish' class. A total of 14 of these handsome engines were built before their designer moved on to the production of the first '196' class 4-6-0s which were basically 'fish' class engines fitted with 6ft 9in wheels built for comparison purposes and tried against the same designer's 4-4-2s on express work.

Over the next 15 years the GCR went on to add 46 more 4-6-0s to their fleet of six different classes, perhaps the most famous of which were the 'Sir Sam Fay' passenger versions which first saw the light of day in 1912 and which became well known for some very fast main line running. Other designs were designated for fast goods duties and had driving wheels of 5ft 3in diameter while mixed traffic versions were equipped with 5ft 7in or 5ft 8in 'drivers'. There was little consistency between batches though as five batches had two outside cylinders, two had inside cylinders and six engines had both!

The same year as the Great Central produced its first 4-6-0 the Caledonian Railway produced its first example, specifically for use on the Callander and Oban line, which had many gradients of 1-in-60 or more and abounded in severe curves. For 20 years or more inside-cylinder 4-4-0s had been adequate for this work but increasing numbers of tourists meant that trains were becoming longer and heavier and beyond the capabilities of the existing locomotives.

JF McIntosh came up with a 4-6-0 with surprisingly small wheels, at 5ft diameter and a boiler and firebox arrangement which would on the face of it have been too small for the task at hand. However, the Oban line was undulating in character and so the boiler was not required to continuously supply large quantities of steam and in consequence the nine 'Oban Bogies' were a huge success and were masters of the line for the next quarter of a century. McIntosh used the same wheel arrangement the following year for his huge express engines which were specifically designed for hauling the Caledonian's crack expresses from England. These trains were also increasing in weight, largely due to the introduction of corridor coaches, and were getting beyond what the current 4-4-0s could cope with. What resulted were two huge engines, numbered 49 and 50, which dwarfed most contemporary designs but which were able to haul expresses unaided up Beattock yet still run at speeds of up to almost 80mph.

> "The Highland Railway introduced Britain's first 4-6-0."
>
> **EVAN GREEN-HUGHES**

Another batch of express 4-6-0s was built in 1906 with four being allocated to Glasgow, Perth and Carlisle. These were allocated the heaviest duties and one of them 903 *Cardean* achieved fame for being the regular engine used on a daily train of 305 tons of West Coast Joint Stock for more than ten years. Another of the batch, 907, also achieved fame, but for the wrong reasons, when it was written off in the 1915 Quintinshill disaster.

Two further 4-6-0s were introduced by the Caledonian in 1906. The '908s' were small wheeled versions of the 'Cardeans' for the Clyde Coast and Glasgow-Perth expresses while the '918s' were in effect large boilered versions of the 'Oban Bogies' designed for goods work. In 1914 William Pickersgill was brought in to succeed McIntosh and after that the Caledonian reverted to building 4-4-0s.

The Swindon approach

Apart from the Highland Railway and the NER only the GWR possessed a 4-6-0 at the turn of »

Stanier's 'Black Five' is often viewed as the ultimate mixed traffic 4-6-0. 'Black Five' 5381 nears Brinklow, north of Rugby, with an Up milk train on September 23 1937. T.G. Hepburn/Rail Archive Stephenson.

the century, but this machine was very different from what was to follow. The solitary example was numbered 36 and was constructed in 1896 for the purpose of hauling heavy freight through the Severn Tunnel. This two-cylinder locomotive was designed by William Dean and was fitted with double frames, having driving wheels of 4ft 7½ in diameter and was by all accounts a very capable machine. However it always remained a prototype and lasted for only nine years before being withdrawn.

The Great Western's move towards 4-6-0s really started with the appointment of George Jackson Churchward in 1902. As has been well documented Churchward was very interested in locomotive development in other parts of the country and indeed in other parts of the world and he must have noted the excellent work being done by the 'ten wheelers' in the USA and by similarly laid out machines in the rest of the UK.

As assistant to William Dean he had already

LNWR Claughton 4-6-0 1914 *Patriot* climbs Camden bank with the Down 'Corridor' from Euston to Glasgow/Edinburgh in 1921. This train was later named the 'Mid-day Scot' in 1927. Rail Archive Stephenson.

Thompson's 'B1' 4-6-0s began entering traffic during the Second World War and were designed to be both simple to build and maintain. On August 3 1957 61201 climbs Ancaster bank with a Mablethorpe-Nottingham holiday express in fine style. T.G. Hepburn/Rail Archive Stephenson.

been working on his own designs and in consequence his first 4-6-0 which carried the number 100 appeared in February 1902. This was a very simple outside cylinder machine with a domeless parallel boiler and Stephenson valve gear. The parallel boiler was soon replaced with a superheated taper design based on American practice. Two more prototypes followed in 1903, both with taper boilers, and the final one of these formed the basis of what was to become the 'Saint' Class.

Following on from this Churchward began to develop his range of engines which used a number of standard parts, such as boilers, cylinders and motion but at first he was not completely satisfied that the 4-6-0 offered significant advantages and as a result some of his engines were built as 4-4-2s. However trials soon proved the superiority of the engines with six driving wheels and from that point on the 4-4-2s were discontinued.

The 'Star' class was the next incarnation of the 4-6-0 from the Great Western but this time with four cylinders and designed for express passenger work. This class laid down the foundation for a long line of four-cylinder express machines which culminated in the 'Kings' and which satisfied the express passenger needs of the Great Western lines right until the end of steam.

For mixed traffic the GWR relied on 2-6-0s for many years but increasing loads in the early 1920s caused then Chief Mechanical Engineer Charles Collett to have a rethink. For experimental purposes he rebuilt 2925 *Saint Martin* with smaller driving wheels, so as to be suitable for goods as well as passenger work. A better cab was fitted too. What emerged was the 'Hall' class, which eventually extended to 259 engines and was one of the outstanding 4-6-0 designs of the century. The GWR also produced designs such as the 'Manor' for specific duties, in this case where lighter axleloads were required.

Pushing the limits

While a great deal of attention has been directed at the Great Western Railway and its 4-6-0s other companies were producing locomotives designed to push the type to its limit. In 1908 George Hughes of the Lancashire and Yorkshire Railway produced the first of two very large four cylinder express passenger locomotives with the mammoth tractive effort of 27,157lbs. These were for heavy trains between Manchester, Leeds, Hull and Sheffield but they suffered from mechanical problems, high coal consumption and poor availability and as a result they were all withdrawn by the First World War and rebuilt.

The Great Eastern Railway had a happier relationship with the 4-6-0, introducing the type in 1911, with 1500 being the first of the 'S69' class. These inside cylinder engines were very handsome indeed and had performance to match their good looks. They were used to haul expresses from Liverpool Street and replaced the 'Claud Hamiltons' and eventually there were 71 of them in service. These were very long-lived

> "The GWR built specific 4-6-0 designs for specific duties"
>
> **EVAN GREEN-HUGHES**

engines and were reclassified 'B12' by the London North Eastern Railway (LNER) following the 1923 grouping and lasted well into British Railways days.

During his time at the London and South Western Railway (LSWR) Dugald Drummond also introduced the 4-6-0 south of the Thames with 330-335 appearing in 1907. These were apparently not successful engines and neither were the next four classes but whatever the issues were they had all been sorted out by the time the 'Paddlebox' 'T14s' were introduced in 1911. These were four cylinder monsters with 200psi boilers and a tractive effort of 25,177lbs and proved moderately successful, lasting into British Railways days, but gaining a reputation for excessive coal and water consumption.

And so it was that within 20 years the number of 4-6-0s at work in the UK had risen from 22 at the turn of the century to no fewer than 976. This number was set to rise dramatically over the next few years as the type found increasing favour firstly as an express passenger design and later as a maid-of-all-work.

As previously intimated the Great Western Railway had embraced the idea of the 4-6-0 wholeheartedly but another railway which had adopted the type was the London and North Western Railway which had begun to build compound 4-6-0s in 1903 with limited success. A simplified design, which was basically an enlarged version of the 'Precursor' 4-4-0, emerged from Crewe in 1904 and proved very successful on the West Coast Main Line, so much so that eventually the company had a total of 420 of them on its books. The ultimate development of this design was the 'Claughton' which was to all intents and purposes the LNWR's version of the GWR's 'Star' and used on similar duties.

Grouping developments

By 1928 Britain's railways had been amalgamated into four organisations, one of which was the London Midland & Scottish Railway (LMS), a company woefully short of adequate motive »

The Drummond four-cylinder 'T14' 4-6-0s earned themselves the nickname 'Paddleboxes' due to the smokebox and steam pipe casing design. Rebuilt 'T14' 446 waits to leave London Waterloo with a Southampton Terminus via Alton train in 1937. Lewis Coles/Rail Archive Stephenson.

power. By this time the 'Claughtons' were not up to the job and usually had to be double-headed while the former Midland Railway had nothing better than a series of 4-4-0s for its fastest trains.

In desperation the LMS borrowed a 'Castle' 4-6-0 from the GWR and this led to a decision to build an express three-cylinder 4-6-0 which was ordered from the North British Engine Co with the resulting 'Royal Scot' class becoming the start of a dynasty of 4-6-0s to be constructed for the LMS. So good was the 'Royal Scot' that eventually some of the 'Claughtons' were rebuilt to a similar pattern to become the slightly smaller 'Patriots'.

It was shortly after this that the line of GWR 4-6-0s and the extensive line of LMS 4-6-0s came together for William Stanier was headhunted from the GWR's Swindon Works to take charge of locomotive development at LMS's Crewe Works. On his arrival he realised that there was a need for a powerful mixed traffic 4-6-0 and so he set about designing what was in effect an LMS version of the GWR's 'Hall' class. Although many ideas were carried on from the Swindon product the engine had to be completely redesigned due to the more restrictive northern loading gauge but what emerged was a machine that was even better than the original, having a boiler working at 225psi supplying two outside cylinders of 18½in x 28in and driving wheels of 6ft in diameter. This class – the Stanier 'Black Five' - was eventually to number 842 and was to continue in production until 1951 with many detail variations between batches.

Stanier continued his developments with his three-cylinder 'Jubilee' but he also modified the 'Royal Scot' and 'Patriots' using similar GWR-style taper boilers and in many ways he continued the development of the 4-6-0, which some say had stagnated at Swindon once a set of standard designs had been worked out.

As might be expected other railways had their equivalent of the 'Hall' and the 'Black Five' with one of the most successful being the London and North Eastern Railway (LNER) 'B1' designed by Edward Thompson and which first saw the light of day in 1942. This was the first 4-6-0 for the LNER since the grouping to have only two cylinders and was designed to be as simple and cheap to construct as possible due to restrictions on materials caused by the war. 'B1s' operated all over the LNER with considerable success, although they are said to have suffered from inferior ride quality. Ultimately 410 entered traffic with some built after the nationalisation of the railways.

The final generation

Although designs such as the 'B1', 'Hall' and 'Black Five' continued in production following

Robinson developed a series of 4-6-0s for the Great Central Railway including the elegant 'B2' class. 425 *City of Manchester* passes Woolmer Green with the 'Sheffield Pullman' from London King's Cross in 1924. Robert Brookman/Rail Archive Stephenson.

Churchward's 'Saint' 4-6-0 for the GWR was a big step forward in locomotive development. In 1925 'Saint' 2902 *Lady of the Lake* waits to leave Paddington with an express. Rail Archive Stephenson.

nationalisation, British Railways, under Robert Riddles, eventually replaced them with two 'Standard' designs of 4-6-0, one in class four and one in class five. These locomotives were heavily influenced by LMS practice, with 172 '5MTs' being built and 80 of the slightly smaller '4MTs'. However by this time the days of the 4-6-0 were almost over. Progressive designers were moving on to the 4-6-2 for express mixed traffic work while others saw the wholesale replacement of the steam fleet by diesels as the only way forward. As it was many 4-6-0s continued to give reliable service until the final days of steam and it was indeed fitting that 'Black Fives' were amongst those used on both the last day and on the commemorative specials.

The 4-6-0 configuration provided sure-footed locomotives capable of a multitude of tasks right from freight work to the fastest expresses. Variations in driving wheel sizes and detail arrangement allowed for locomotives to be able to enjoy a fine range of activities and the design was to dominate the number of locomotives built in the second quarter of the 20th century. In the UK, just as in Europe and America, it was perhaps the most versatile wheel arrangement ever used. ∎

Caledonian Railway '908' 4-6-0 914 waits to leave Glasgow Central with a Clyde Coast train in 1912.
Rail Archive Stephenson.

WEATHERING

Back in the day

TIM SHACKLETON explores how steam locomotives looked and weathered in pre-war years – very differently, he suggests, to how most modellers imagine they do.

'THE PAST IS ANOTHER COUNTRY,' wrote L.P. Hartley in *The Go-Between*. 'They do things differently there…' Nowadays there can be few active modellers who have memories of railways in the inter-war period, that glorious era of the 'Big Four' when trains were clean and punctual, when stations were ablaze with colourful flower baskets, enamel signs and posters and the countryside was dotted with picturesque cottages painted in attractive pastel shades.

But was it really like this? Did locomotives and railway stations look as clean and tidy as they do in, say, *Foyle's War* or *Downton Abbey* and the other TV costume dramas from which we seem to draw our inspiration? Did every railway bridge really have a gaily-painted bus or a traction engine perpetually trundling over it? Was every coal yard a kaleidoscope of red, yellow, green and blue private-owner wagons? The answer is, probably not.

Until the 1950s heavy industry dominated whole swathes of the country, coal was the universal fuel and anti-pollution legislation was virtually non-existent. Rural railways were run on a shoestring, elbow grease alone kept most things clean (or not) and outward appearances mattered far less than they do today.

I have looked at a great many colour photographs of Britain in the 1920s, 1930s and 1940s – yes, they exist, and in surprising numbers – and my over-riding impression is of a dingy, down-at-heel, tired-looking world very far removed from the chocolate-box imagery so beloved of TV producers - and modellers. For this *Yearbook* project I wanted to look at how things really were. Two books that have long been an inspiration for me in recreating this dowdy pre-war world are *The Big Four in Colour* by David Jenkinson (Atlantic) and *Britain: The First Colour Photographs* by Roger A Freeman (Blandford). Both are easy to find at knock-down prices in charity shops or on Abe Books - www.abebooks.co.uk. If you model this period or are even vaguely interested in it, I suggest you get hold of them as they make for fascinating viewing. ∎

The overwhelming evidence from photographs and film footage is that the inter-war period was anything but the chocolate-box idyll we see on television, and the Victorian and Edwardian eras even less so. These two locomotives might not have crossed paths in real life, but their appearance after weathering suggests an era which many see in a different, cleaner, light.

WHAT WE USED		
PRODUCT	MANUFACTURER	CAT NO.
Fuel Stains	AK-Interactive	AK025
Frame Dirt	Lifecolor	UA719
Worn Black	Lifecolor	UA734
Burned Black	Lifecolor	UA736
Streaking Grime for US vehicles	MIG Ammo	1207
Engine Grime	MIG Ammo	1407
Fuel Stains	MIG Ammo	1409
Grey Filter	MIG Ammo	1505
Deep Grey	MIG Ammo	1602
Black Night	MIG Ammo	1611
Black (powder)	MIG Ammo	3001
Medium Rust (powder)	MIG Ammo	3005
Track Rust (powder)	MIG Ammo	3008
Gun Metal (powder)	MIG Ammo	3009
Old Grease (powder)	MIG Ammo	GP11

WEATHERING PRE-WAR LOCOMOTIVES

1 Our project locomotives are two stunning models from Bachmann and Hornby respectively – LNER 'D11/2' 4-4-0 6385 *Luckie Mucklebackit* and Drummond '700' 0-6-0 695 of the Southern Railway. Glistening in the sunshine, it's hardly surprising that locomotives of the inter-war period are so attractive to modellers.

2 Why am I using so many different weathering products on this project? Because it's easier this way! Unless you're blessed with a high level of skill at blending, it's very difficult to restrict yourself to just a handful of base colours. I use different products for different purposes – washes and filters to tone down what's underneath, enamel and acrylic paint to build up layers of colour, weathering powders to add fine details and tonal variation. It's a far cry from the all-in-one universal 'weathering tint'!

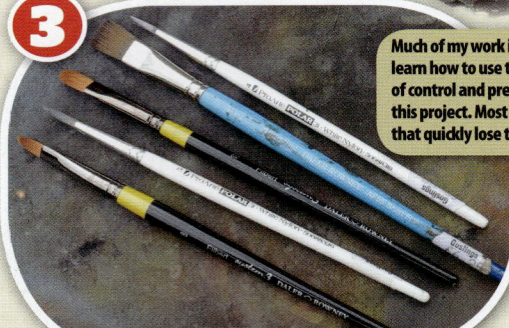

3 Much of my work is and always has been done with paintbrushes. If you learn how to use them properly, they give you an extraordinary degree of control and precision. Note the different sizes and shapes I used for this project. Most cost a fiver or less, though I avoid cheap paintbrushes that quickly lose their shape and moult half their bristles.

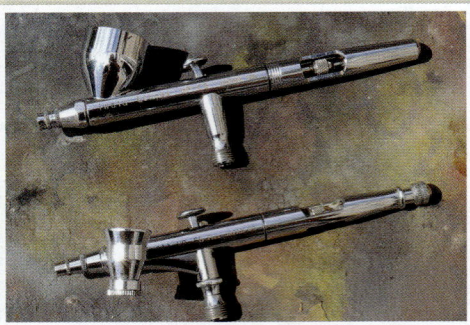

4 These are the two Iwata airbrushes I used for this project – an Eclipse CS for the delicate stuff and an HP-SB Plus for the even more delicate stuff. Budget airbrushes – and I have a few – have no subtlety and there is no point trying to use them for this kind of weathering.

5 Much of the initial work is done using enamel washes from the MIG Ammo range, specifically Black Night (1611) and Engine Grime (1407). You can always mix your own but these high-quality commercial products are just the right consistency for brushing and give you consistent colours. Not everyone has the knack of mixing paint to the exact shade they want.

6 Black locomotives go grey when they're not cleaned, so I tested out Engine Grime by lightly brushing it on to the cabsides and tender rears, then taking most of it off again. The wash will help discolour the underlying paintwork, as well as collecting in corners exactly as accumulated dirt does on the real thing.

Hornby's Drummond '700' 0-6-0 looks absolutely splendid in lined black, a livery style that was discontinued in 1936. By the standards of the day I'd suggest this was actually quite clean for a goods engine – they got a lot dirtier than this, but the really decrepit look was more a wartime characteristic.

WEATHERING

7 This is how to put on a colour wash. Using a broad, flat brush I flood the bodywork – in this case the 'D11s' tender side sheets – with an initial application of grime. The less you put on, the less there will be to take off and the wastage will consequently be lower.

8 Dampen the brush in dean thinners, wipe it almost dry (not on a paper towel or anything fluffy – dragging it between your finger and thumb is as good as anything) and then brush away the surplus colour wash. Continue to do this – cleaning and recharging the brush as necessary – until you have the effect you want.

9 How much you take off depends on the kind of result you want. You can never quite go back to the original pristine finish, but reducing the wash down to a hint of gentle discoloration – as here – looks remarkably effective. If you want your engine to look more dirty, don't take so much off.

10 Hand-brushing a thin wash of Engine Grime on to the running plate. The Daler-Rowney 'Acquafine' brushes that I've used for some years are now discontinued but I find the 'Polar' range of synthetic brushes from ProArte work very well in modelling applications. The brushes are tough and keep their shape well.

11 Even in pre-war colour photographs you can see subtle variations in the way different parts of a steam locomotive become discoloured. To paint the boiler I've switched to another Mig AMMO shade, designed for creating streaking effects on modern American military vehicles (1207).

12 Working in strong light – so I can see the textures starting to form – I'm soft-brushing the streaking wash on the boiler, coaxing it into semi-invisibility. The brush is lightly dampened with dean white spirit from the little jar on the left.

13 A touch of Black Night panel wash on the 'D11s' front bufferbeam. It flashes over the surface and collects in the various angles, emphasizing relief detail and the build-up of oily dirt in hard-to-reach areas.

14 All I've done so far is to put a colour wash or two over the 'Director' and take most of it off again. Although still very much a lined-black locomotive, it's a very different shade of black to the Drummond '700' class behind, which at this stage has hardly been touched.

15 Just to ring the changes, the Drummond 'Black Motor' gets an initial wash of Ammo Deep Grey. This stuff is easy enough to put on – the skill lies in the discrimination and subtlety you employ in working it to create a believable surface finish. You can slosh it on with abandon but from this point on you need to treat it with respect – and the delicacy of a watercolourist.

WEATHERING PRE-WAR LOCOMOTIVES

16 Fortunately it doesn't take long to acquire the necessary skills. Here I'm flicking the still-wet paint with a No 5 candle-flame brush - you need large-ish brushes for this kind of work. All the time I'm reducing the amount of paint on the model and creating interesting, prototypically inspired weathering patterns. I'm looking for a measure of unevenness in the surface texture, but nothing in any way obvious.

17 Having left the enamel washes to dry overnight I've begun gentle airbrushing with acrylic paints from LifeColor's useful set of Black Rubber Shades. Worn Black (UA734) is particularly good for cab roofs while the slightly warmer-tinged Burned Black (UA736) works well on smokeboxes. You only need a touch of paint in the right place for the model to start to come to life.

18 LifeColor's Rail Weathering set is one I come back to time and again. I toned down the wheels and underframes using a combination of Frame Dirt (UA719) and the ubiquitous Burned Black. Just a fine mist of discolouration is all you need – save the really heavy weathering for wartime or the end-of-steam era.

19 To get the oily steel look on coupling rods I paint them with Fuel Stains, available both from AK-Interactive (AK025) and Ammo (1409). I also used some on the tender axleboxes of the 'Director'. The windows need a wipe with airbrush cleaner!

20 Coal is a highly acidic mineral with abrasive qualities – that's why paint quickly scrapes off coal bunkers and corrosion sets in. I wanted to use weathering powders to represent this so the first step was to carefully airbrush the area with Ammo's acrylic Rust Primer (2006). This gives a much tougher and more resilient surface to work on than ordinary acrylic colours would provide.

21 The Mig AMMO weathering powders are as good as it gets. To enhance the subtlety I used no fewer than four different colours, applied with a stabbing, stippling motion – in order of quantities used, Medium Rust (3005), Track Rust (3008), Gun Metal (3009) and Black (3001). If you're using acrylics as a base coat, allow a good 24hr for them to fully harden before applying weathering powders – otherwise the painted surface might start to break up.

22 Once I was happy with the basic application I stroked the powders with my brush to blend them together and soften any edges. The gunmetal colour can be lightly polished to add a delicate sheen to areas where coal would slide down the bunker and abrade the surface. Note how beautifully understated the AMMO rust colours are.

Luckie Mucklebackit sees the cleaner's rag quite frequently but is still every inch the working locomotive and that is the character I wanted to put across. What handsome, elegant engines the 'Directors' were! "There was about Luckie Mucklebackit and her family an appearance of ease, plenty, and comfort" wrote Sir Walter Scott in *The Antiquary*, and this is reflected in the locomotive that carries his character's name.

WEATHERING

23 I've used the same colours around the water filler and rear coal bulkhead, this time with the emphasis on Black - which is actually an extremely dark brown. Even without coal, the tender is starting to look the part…

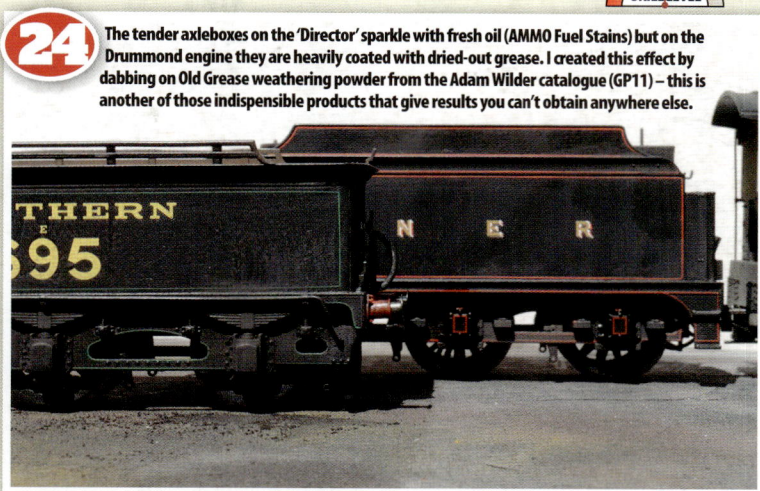

24 The tender axleboxes on the 'Director' sparkle with fresh oil (AMMO Fuel Stains) but on the Drummond engine they are heavily coated with dried-out grease. I created this effect by dabbing on Old Grease weathering powder from the Adam Wilder catalogue (GP11) – this is another of those indispensible products that give results you can't obtain anywhere else.

25 Feeling they were still a bit too black, I lightened the tone of the '700s' boiler and running plate with a gentle mist of a MIG Ammo grey filter (1505). Designed for AFVs in desert sand colour, it works equally well with 'Black Motors'. At this point I decided that I'd gone about as far as I wanted to go with these two locomotives, so I reached for a hammer…

26 Nothing looks like locomotive coal so much as real coal. I wrap a lump in a plastic bag, park it on the back step and hit it hard with a hammer. Small coal is fine but you don't want many big lumps, which were hard for a fireman to manage.

USEFUL LINKS

■ AK-Interactive	www.ak-interactive.com
■ Lifecolor/Wilder	www.airbrushes.com
■ MIG Ammo	www.migjimenez.com

LIGHTING

CARRIAGE LIGHTING
made simple

Adding interior lights couldn't be simpler with Train-Tech's easy to install battery powered lighting strips. **MIKE WILD** shows how he went about adding lights to Bachmann's 'OO' gauge inspection saloon.

INTERIOR LIGHTS can make a huge difference to a model – and especially if you enjoy running trains after dark. However, lighting projects tend to be left to those with soldering skills as most vehicles will require electrical pick-ups as well as lights.

Thankfully that isn't the only way to go about adding interior lighting. Specialist supplier Train-Tech has produced a range of LED lighting strips which require absolutely no soldering at all. They are self powered with small circular batteries and can be installed in very little time in the majority of current ready-to-run rolling stock.

Train-Tech's three strip pack for 'N' gauge carriages (Cat No. CN200) is the source of materials for this quick workbench project to install interior lighting in the Bachmann London Midland & Scottish Railway inspection saloon. Adding lights is a straightforward process requiring removal of the body – a clip fit to the chassis – and careful positioning of two of the 'N' gauge lighting strips on the underside of the roof. The only other modification was to create clearance space in the internal walls to make sure the body still fitted comfortably onto the chassis.

The simplicity of Train-Tech's lighting strips makes them a joy to install and they have a self timer feature which turns the lights off if the vehicle has been stationary for more than four minutes. Turning the lights back on is handled by a motion sensor so once installed, apart from an occasional battery change, there is no maintenance required either.

The result is a carriage which looks all the better for the addition of interior lights – all this one needs now is a collection of management 'passengers' to complete the picture! ■

WHAT WE USED

PRODUCT	MANUFACTURER	CAT NO.
LMS 50ft inspection saloon, BR maroon	Bachmann	39-779
'N' gauge carriage lighting kit	Train-Tech	CN200

USEFUL LINKS

Bachmann	www.bachmann.co.uk
Train-Tech	www.train-tech.com

PLEASE TURN FOR STEP BY STEP GUIDE

Lighting brings great atmosphere to a model railway. With the station building lit with Woodland Scenics Just-Plug system and station lamps by DCC Concepts, the newly kitted out inspection saloon looks at home.

LIGHTING

INSTALLING LIGHTING IN AN INSPECTION SALOON

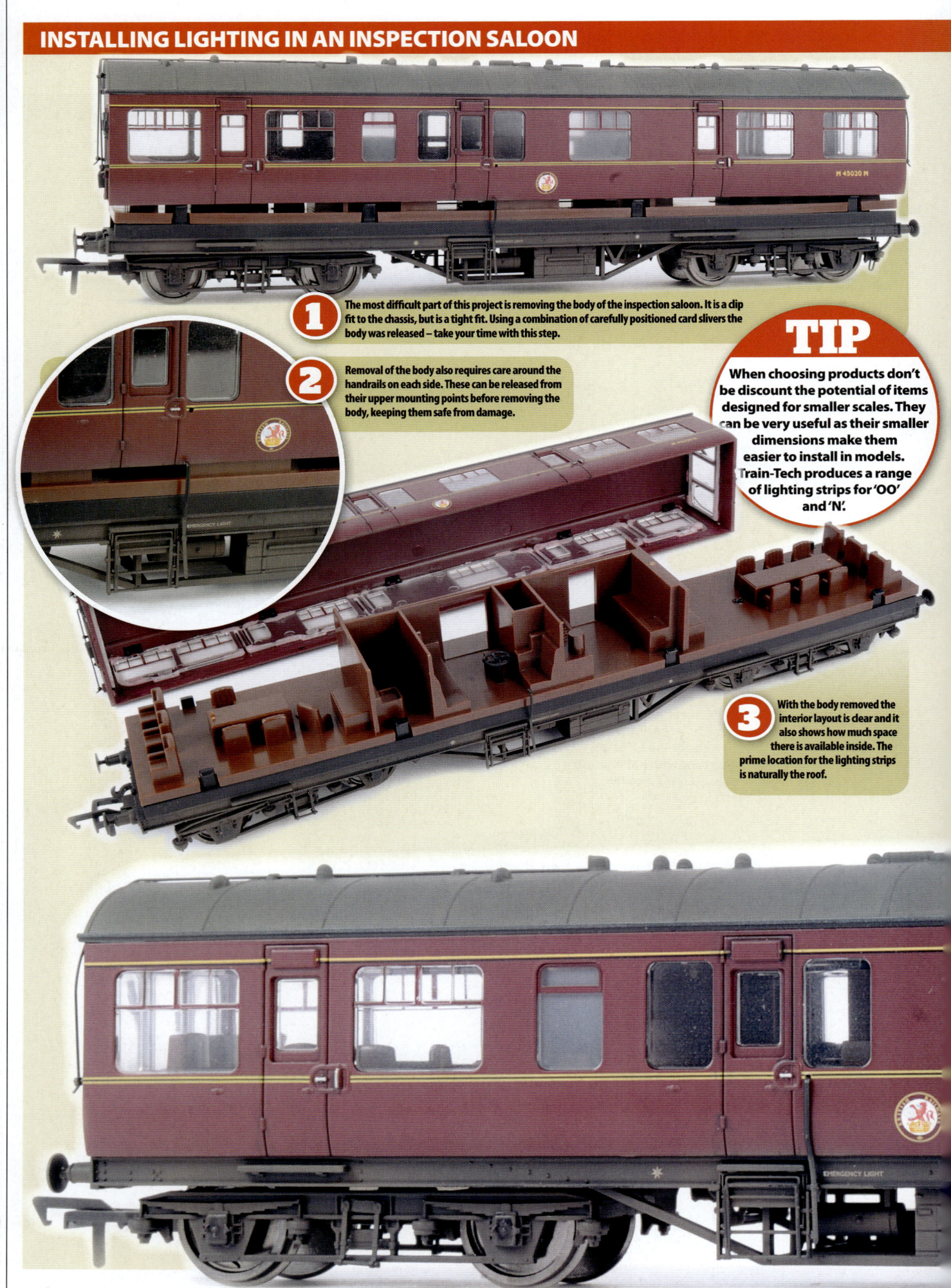

1 The most difficult part of this project is removing the body of the inspection saloon. It is a clip fit to the chassis, but is a tight fit. Using a combination of carefully positioned card slivers the body was released – take your time with this step.

2 Removal of the body also requires care around the handrails on each side. These can be released from their upper mounting points before removing the body, keeping them safe from damage.

TIP When choosing products don't be discount the potential of items designed for smaller scales. They can be very useful as their smaller dimensions make them easier to install in models. Train-Tech produces a range of lighting strips for 'OO' and 'N'.

3 With the body removed the interior layout is clear and it also shows how much space there is available inside. The prime location for the lighting strips is naturally the roof.

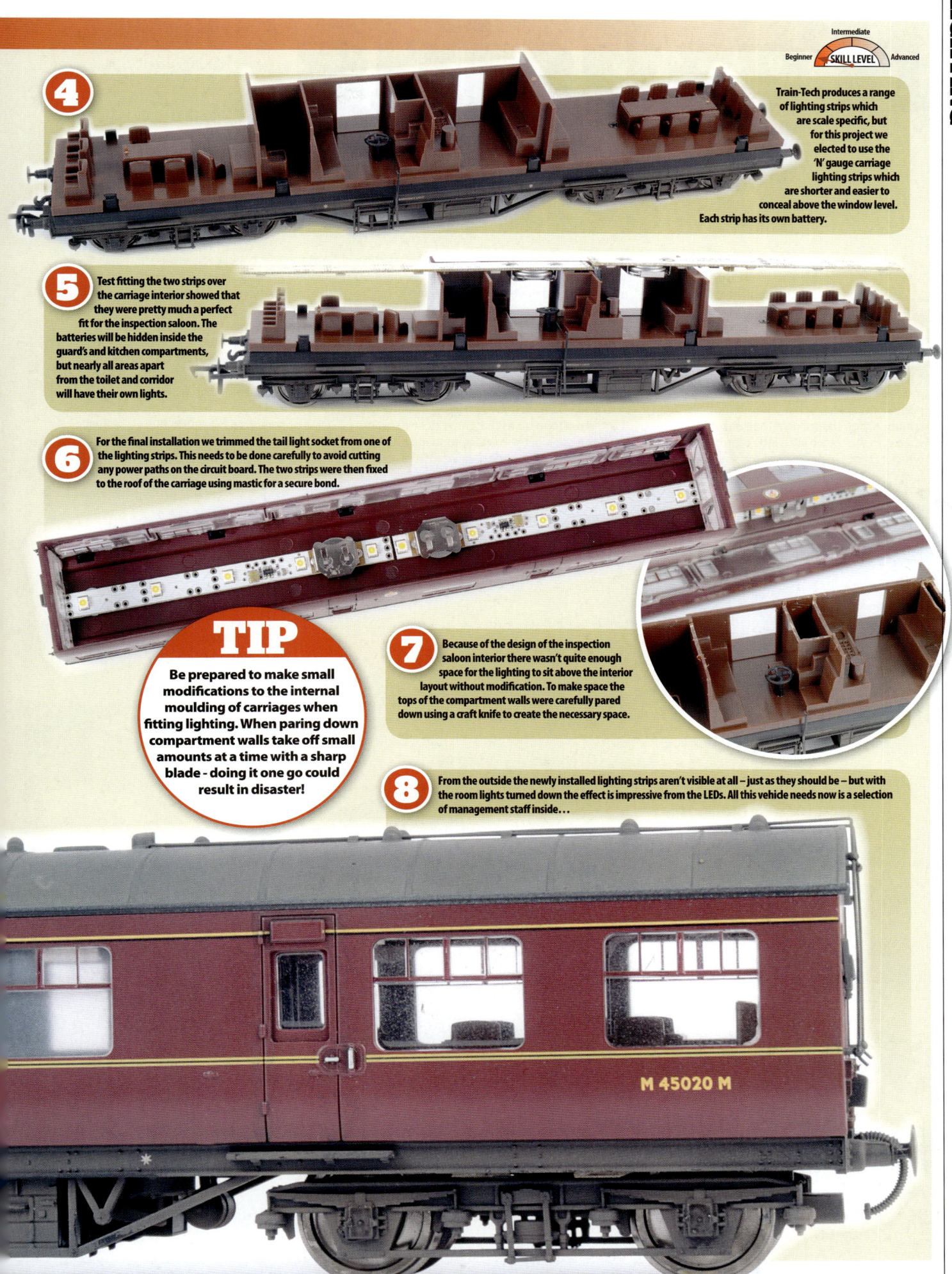

4 Train-Tech produces a range of lighting strips which are scale specific, but for this project we elected to use the 'N' gauge carriage lighting strips which are shorter and easier to conceal above the window level. Each strip has its own battery.

5 Test fitting the two strips over the carriage interior showed that they were pretty much a perfect fit for the inspection saloon. The batteries will be hidden inside the guard's and kitchen compartments, but nearly all areas apart from the toilet and corridor will have their own lights.

6 For the final installation we trimmed the tail light socket from one of the lighting strips. This needs to be done carefully to avoid cutting any power paths on the circuit board. The two strips were then fixed to the roof of the carriage using mastic for a secure bond.

TIP
Be prepared to make small modifications to the internal moulding of carriages when fitting lighting. When paring down compartment walls take off small amounts at a time with a sharp blade - doing it one go could result in disaster!

7 Because of the design of the inspection saloon interior there wasn't quite enough space for the lighting to sit above the interior layout without modification. To make space the tops of the compartment walls were carefully pared down using a craft knife to create the necessary space.

8 From the outside the newly installed lighting strips aren't visible at all – just as they should be – but with the room lights turned down the effect is impressive from the LEDs. All this vehicle needs now is a selection of management staff inside...

MODELLING IN 'N'

N'gauging interest

'N' gauge is growing in popularity so **NIGEL BURKIN** explains how to make a start in British outline 'N' gauge modelling and why he made the switch.

MINIATURISATION is a fact of life and as pressure for living space intensifies, particularly in cities, the room available to pursue a space-grabbing hobby such as railway modelling becomes more and more scarce.

It is no surprise that 'N' gauge – 2mm:1ft scale models running on approximately 9mm track – is popular in Japan as it has allowed modellers to continue their passion in remarkably confined spaces. In the UK we are a little more fortunate when it comes to finding space for a model railway because our homes are generally larger than those found in crowded Japanese cities. So space can be a driver for those looking to build a model railway in a short space – but there's many more possibilities in this diminutive scale.

I switched to 'N' gauge (1:148 scale) and 'N' scale (1:160 scale) in 2004 for several different reasons. 'N' scale allowed me to model more North American railroad in the same space than 'HO' scale (3.5mm:1ft) would allow. With 'N' scale, I could run long trains that came close to giving an impression of the massive tonnage routinely hauled by North American railroads in a scenic setting that could be modelled to match the country in south west Montana. A larger scale would not have made that possible in the space available. Work started on that layout in 2009 and continues to this day.

After dabbling in British outline 'N' gauge (which has a different scale to North American 'N') for a while, I built two portable British outline layouts, including Wheal Annah which has been featured in *Hornby Magazine* and one representing main line operations modelled in the space that an 'OO' gauge modeller would be hard pressed to squeeze in a small branch line terminus.

A smaller gauge offers the chance to model more railway. The 'N' gauge Wheal Annah project features several china clay dries, a station and a short mineral branch in an area measuring 100cm x 50cm.

Better models

For years the quality of models in 'N' gauge was a problem. Detailing was relatively poor, choice limited and the mechanisms not all that smooth. The new products from Bachmann's Graham Farish arm and Dapol have transformed that perception with models of a quality you'd have struggled to find in larger scales 30 years ago. Trade support from smaller manufacturers and the N Gauge Society is also on the increase.

Newcomers to the hobby are enjoying the benefits of smaller layouts and more railway in a smaller area. Certainly, I have found a great deal of satisfaction from the two 'N' gauge layouts I have constructed so far!

After years modelling in 4mm:1ft scale I switched to 'N' gauge in search of a challenge, which was ultimately put to the test with Wheal Annah in the pages of *Hornby Magazine*. It is a compact layout with tight shunting moves demanding pretty precise operation to realise its operating potential – almost a shunting puzzle layout. I had already proven the competence of current 'N' gauge models in a main line setting. Could the off-the-shelf Dapol and Bachmann Graham Farish products achieve the same level of performance on a compact end to end layout as 'OO' gauge ones?

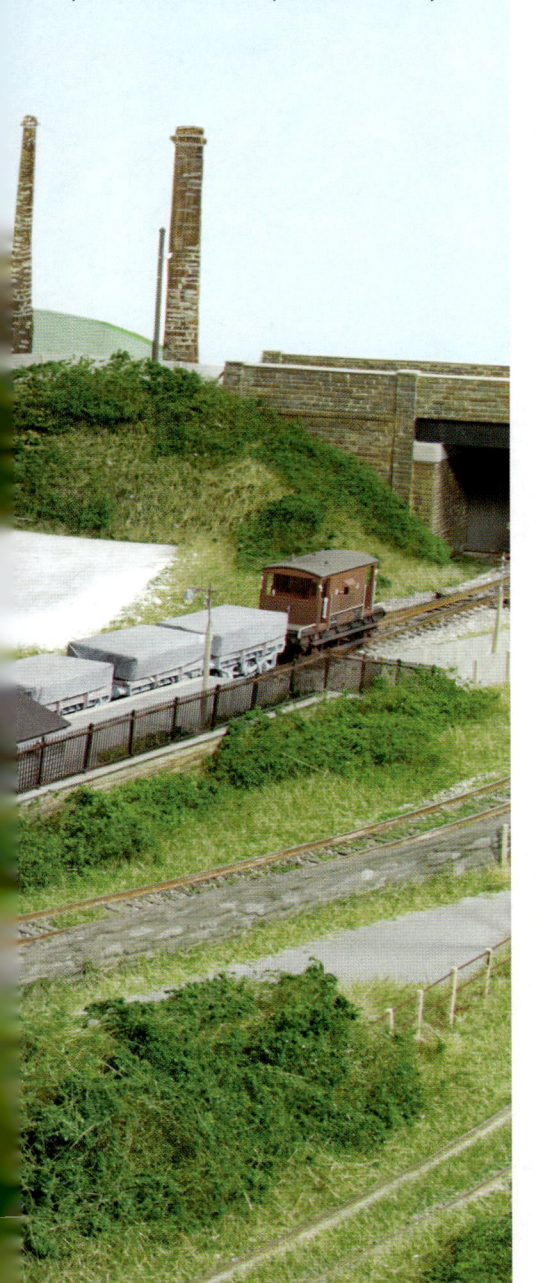

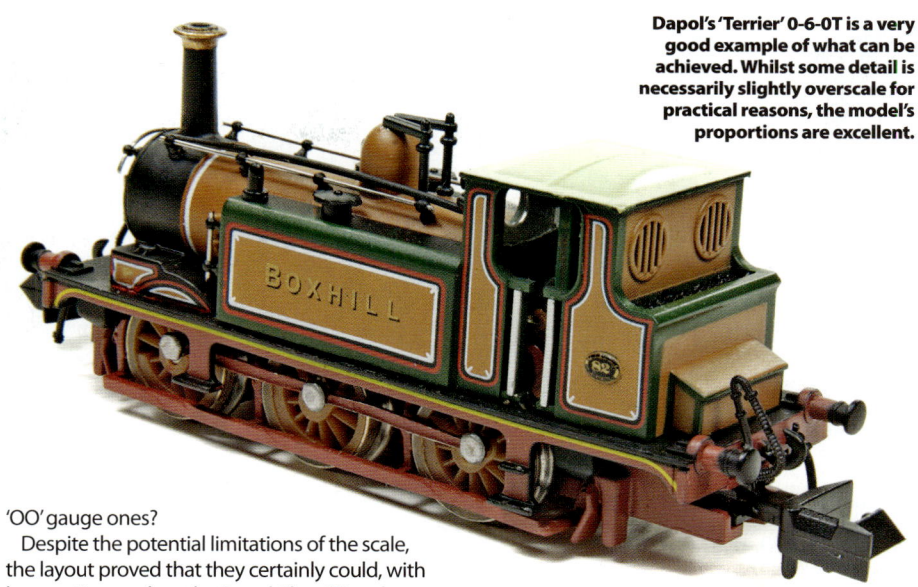

Despite the potential limitations of the scale, the layout proved that they certainly could, with locomotives such as the Dapol Class 22 and Class 52 achieving silky slow speed running to the point where the spokes and weight-saving holes of the respective locomotives' wheels are easily seen rotating and without any hesitation or stalling. Wagons from the Dapol, Peco and Graham Farish ranges performed well over Peco Streamline track with no derailments. The days of poor performance clearly are long gone.

What is 'N' gauge?

Like many things in British outline modelling, 'N' gauge is a workable compromise between actual scale and track gauge which is pragmatically accepted by the majority of modellers in the interests of having a working layout. Commercial British 'N' gauge models are built to a scale ratio of 1:148 which is not technically 2mm:1ft but a tad more - 2mm:1ft equates to a scale of 1:152.

They are designed to run on track with a gauge of 9mm – the space between the rails - an historical compromise with a complex history which dates back to a range of models produced to a scale smaller than 'OO' gauge in the 1950s. A track gauge of (roughly) 9mm was chosen for a range of models produced in the UK called 'Treble O' or 'OOO' which were unmotorised.

In Europe, the same developments were taking place with electric 'N' gauge models being produced initially by Arnold Rapido (which also developed the 'Rapido' coupling) and eventually by other companies such as Minitrix and Fleischmann. Again, 9mm gauge track was chosen as the standard track gauge.

Divergence in the development of the now fledgling 'N' gauge system saw the adoption of a scale of 1:160 in Europe to better match the choice of 9mm for the track gauge - a combination which is now generally referred to as 'N' scale.

So, how did British outline modellers end up with a scale of 1:148 instead of 1:160? The answer lies in the loading gauge of the full size railways. Loading gauges in Europe and North America are considerably more generous than in the UK for the same track gauge. As the scale grew in popularity during the 1960s, available electric motor technology was not as refined as it is today. Whilst the smallest motors available at the time would fit models of European locomotives, they were too large for UK prototypes when modelled to 1:160 scale.

To compensate, manufacturers expanded the size of British outline models to 1:148 scale to accommodate the motors of the time, a compromise we live with today, even though electric motors are now smaller and more efficient.

The gauge to scale compromise remains simply because there is little commercial incentive by mainstream manufacturers to correct the scale compromise by producing British outline models to 1:160 scale to match commercial 9mm »

Dapol's 'Terrier' 0-6-0T is a very good example of what can be achieved. Whilst some detail is necessarily slightly overscale for practical reasons, the model's proportions are excellent.

At the other end of the scale, the most up to date diesel locomotives are available in 'N' gauge including the Class 70 diesel locomotive produced in 'N' and 'OO' gauges by Bachmann. Modern 'N' gauge toolings and livery application are excellent and larger locomotive models such as the Class 70 are easy to fit with DCC decoders.

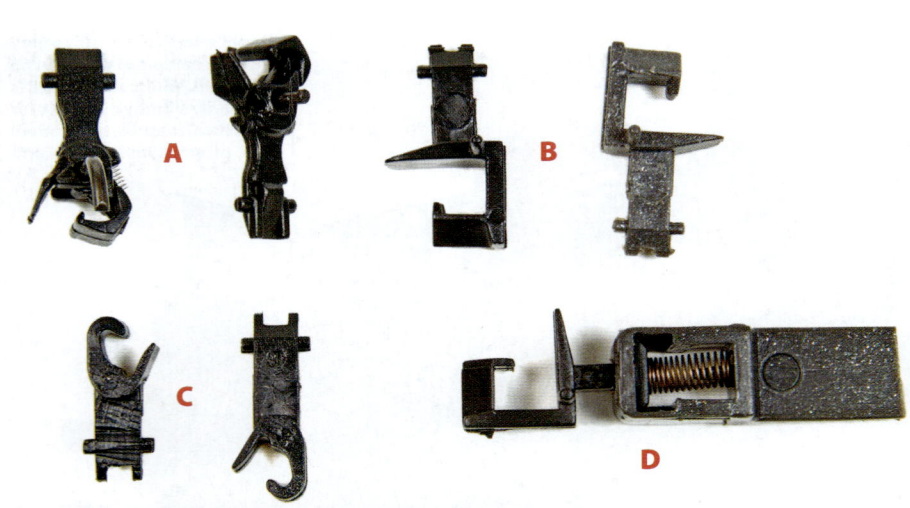

MODELLING IN 'N'

A **B**

C **D**

The adoption of standard (NEM) coupling pockets means that the standard type fitted to most British 'N' gauge models can be easily swapped for different coupling types as long as they have the compatible shank. Examples include the Dapol Easy-Fit coupling (A) standard Rapido coupling (B) together with a variety of dummy couplings (C) which are now available with the correct fitting. They contrast with the Rapido coupling and spring assembly of old (D).

gauge track systems which are readily available with a wide range of crossings and turnouts at a reasonable price. It is also unlikely that any mainstream manufacturer will approach the compromise from the opposite direction and invest in a 9.42mm gauge track system to better match the model scale of 1:148. Any scale to gauge change at this stage would discourage modellers and initiate a long transition period which might prove costly and difficult to manage.

Newcomers to the hobby should always be aware of the slight difference in scale between British outline 'N' gauge and European (together with North American) 'N' scale when it comes to buying items that are absolute in size such as containers, rolling stock, road vehicles and so on. When it comes to layout details such as structures, figures, and scenic details, the scale difference is not so critical and many modellers will willingly use European and American products to complete their layouts.

Start-'N'-g out

When you get started there's the chance of wasting money on false starts, so it pays to do a little research before heading off to the model shop. The starting point for research is to decide what actually interests you. What is it about railway modelling and the wider hobby that appeals? You need to decide on a theme and it can be completely prototypical or freelanced or a bit of both, thinking about location, time period, company you wish to model – and the type of railway: a complex junction station is a much more involved undertaking than a country branch line, but both can be equally satisfying.

Buying the models

Having decided on a theme for your collection it is time to do more practical research. What is available to help you achieve your goals? Virtually any railway era from the 'Big Four' companies to modern day operations can be achieved in 'N' gauge with few gaps thanks to the fairly aggressive model development programmes of both Bachmann, with its Graham Farish brand, and Dapol.

To assist with selecting the correct rolling stock, at least from the Graham Farish range, it is worth visiting the Bachmann website and looking at

Established 'N' gauge modellers have come to enjoy a comparable level of detail on steam locomotives as in 'OO' gauge.

Limitations

All railway modelling is a compromise, whether it's a limit to train length, distances between stations, how sharp the track curves are and how much space is available to create a believable model. 'N' gauge has its own limitations which actually makes it work on one hand, yet require some tinkering and adjustment on the other hand if certain types of railway operation are to be modelled.

Shunting, for example, is a challenge if you stick with the default Rapido couplings offered by the main manufacturers. However, you can change them and run a perfectly good layout: it just takes a little extra work.

An example of how 'N' gauge has improved over the last decade. The old Graham Farish Class 25 model (rear) is slowly being superseded by a new model with dramatically upgraded mouldings and mechanisms (front) together with DCC sockets and working lights.

the Era classifications which offer some idea as to the equipment to choose for a given time period. There is also a great deal of valuable information on the N Gauge Society website which will assist with the selection of appropriate models and equipment.

Dapol is a relatively new entrant in British outline 'N' gauge, developing a high quality range of British outline models including steam, diesel and electric locomotives. Graham Farish is a longer established name in the business and has been producing 'N' gauge models since the early 1970s. It used to be an independent company operating from a small factory in Poole, Dorset. Since its acquisition by Bachmann Europe in 2000, there has been a programme to redevelop much of the former Graham Farish catalogue with better drives, wheels, electronics and hi-fidelity bodyshells featuring much improved levels of detail. Bachmann also offers a range of buildings and details to support the Graham Farish range.

Currently, a transition between those models developed by the independent Graham Farish and the new generation of Bachmann Graham Farish models exists where both standards are still present in the catalogue. Eventually, the »

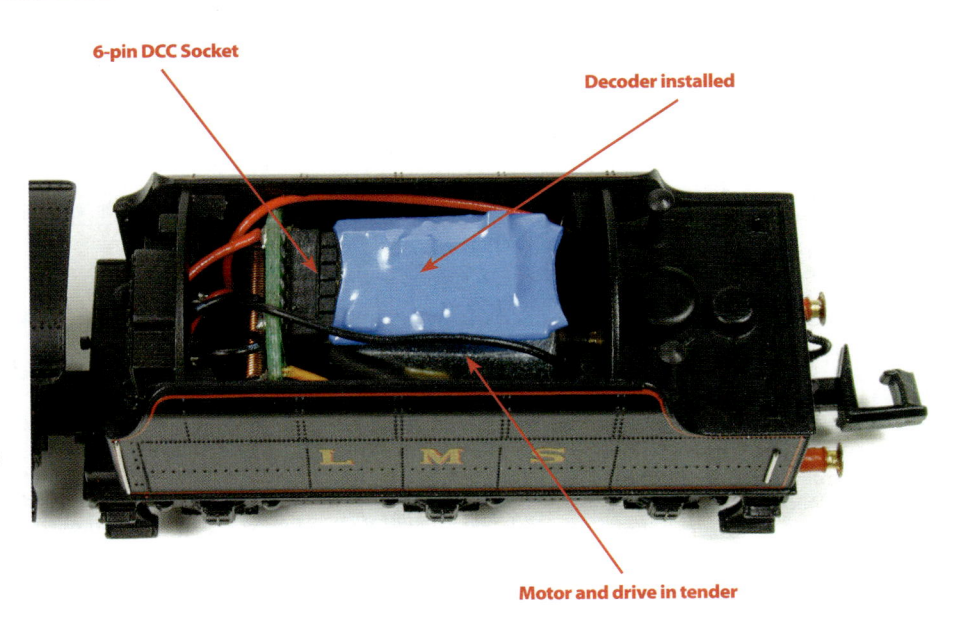

- 6-pin DCC Socket
- Decoder installed
- Motor and drive in tender

Tender drives means that the plug and play NEM-651 6-pin DCC socket is easily incorporated into the design without the issues of space. The coal load of this Graham Farish steam locomotive is simply dropped out to reveal the motor and DCC socket.

As if more proof were needed as to the quality of 'N' gauge models offered today, they can stand some very close up photography. Dapol's Class 121 and 122 single car DMUs are prime examples of 'N' gauge at its best.

company will have worked through what is a very large range to ensure all models are to modern standards. Examples which remain from the former Poole tooling collection include the Class 87 and 90 electric locomotives together with the Class 158 and Class 170 Diesel Multiple Units.

Peco is another important name in the hobby with respect to suitable track systems although it has attempted to dip its toe in the ready-to-run market with some locomotives and an extensive range of wagons. It offers two ready-to-use track systems for 'N' gauge modellers which are available off the shelf at a reasonable cost. The standard system is called Streamline Code 80 track which includes a range of turnouts and crossings. In recent years, a newer universal finescale Code 55 track system was introduced. The code refers to the size of the rail and both track systems feature flat bottom rail.

Whilst on the subject of track, a new development in 'N' gauge track worth investigating is the Code 40 track system in development by a company called Finetrax. Introduced in 2013, the range continues to be developed with track components and kits to 9mm gauge or true 'N' gauge. Furthermore, the Kato Uni-Track system is produced to 9mm gauge and has found favour with many 'N' gauge modellers particularly for its flexibility as a clip together system.

As research moves further away from the mainstream manufacturers, it is possible to find companies that produce products including Ratio for structures and details, Hornby's Lyddle End buildings range, C-Rail Intermodal for modern container operations, Taylor Plastic Models, Wills, Ratio and Springside to mention a few. Vinyl overlay conversions for locomotives and coaching stock are popular in 'N' gauge and such kits are produced by Electra-Railway Graphics. A full list of manufacturers producing models, rolling stock kits, accessories and details for British outline 'N'

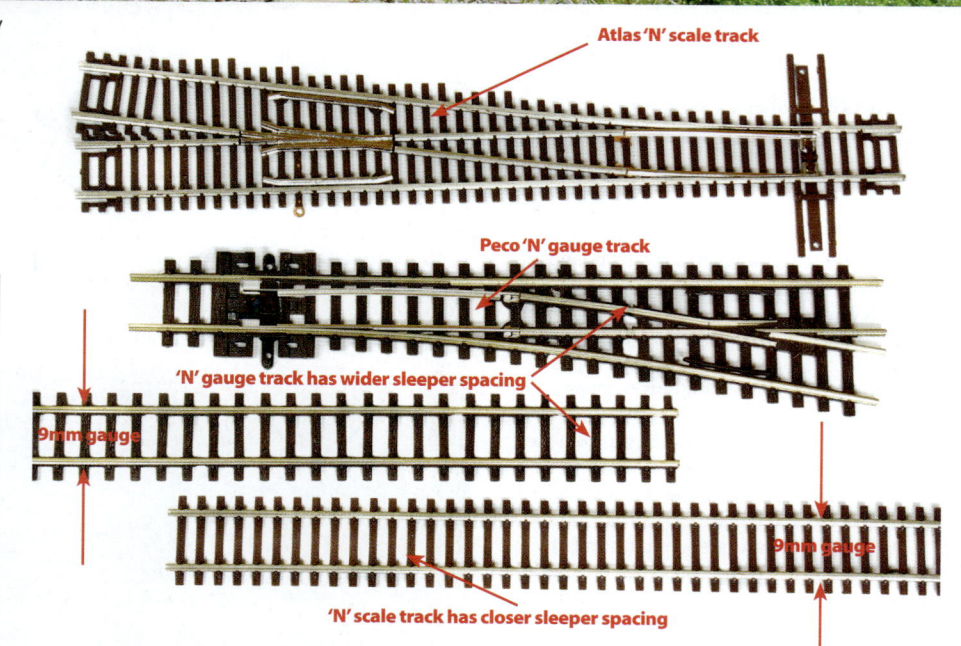

'N' gauge (9mm gauge) track systems are produced for the UK market by Peco. However, there are equivalent systems available from other manufacturers such as Kato, Atlas, and many others which are not necessarily suitable for British outline layouts. For example, the Atlas Code 55 track shown alongside Peco Streamline track in this photograph has 1:160 scale North American sleeper spacing which is too narrow for British track.

Labels: Atlas 'N' scale track; Peco 'N' gauge track; 'N' gauge track has wider sleeper spacing; 9mm gauge; 'N' scale track has closer sleeper spacing; 9mm gauge

The products from the mainstream 'N' gauge manufacturers are designed to work together. A Dapol Class 22 locomotive shunts 'clay hood' wagons which are special edition models commissioned by Kernow Model Rail Centre and produced by Bachmann.

gauge can be found on the N Gauge Society's website.

Naturally, there is a vast amount of modelling material available to 'N' gauge modellers which is not scale-specific including Woodland Scenics, Circuitron Tortoise point motors, DCC Concepts Cobalt point motors, digital control systems and decoders from almost any manufacturer together with general modelling materials such as foam underlay, glues, adhesives, plasticard products - you name it!

It is a matter of selecting the materials to suit the scale. Digital Command Control (DCC) suppliers offer 6-pin decoders to suit most 'N' gauge models or the wired equivalent should you have to consider a hard wire installation. 'N' gauge models will also work with conventional controllers if tackling DCC conversions is not high on your list of priorities. When using scenery products, finer ground cover materials will be more appropriate. It is a matter of personal judgement as to what works for you.

Buying your first equipment

Before investing too much money in the purchase of 'N' gauge equipment, consider buying a small selection of items which could include a couple of locomotives, a handful of rolling stock and some track to experiment with. This is part and parcel of layout concept and design, learning the limitations of the scale and to determine what would and would not be possible on a layout.

You will soon work out that 'N' gauge has its limitations including the continued use of the now long in the tooth Rapido coupling. Although couplings remain a problem in British outline 'N' gauge, the adoption of NEM coupling pockets is making matters considerably easier for modellers, although these aren't fitted to every model. The coupling pockets are standard no matter the manufacturer and will accept a range of couplings with the correct fitting. NEM coupling pockets are introduced as new models are released and include close coupling cams and some alternatives to the Rapido coupling.

Consider building a diorama

Building a small diorama is a low cost way of experimenting with layout construction where mistakes can be easily rectified and are not too expensive. Dioramas do not need to be large – a piece of plywood measuring about 18in x 9in will provide as large an area as necessary to make mistakes and learn some valuable modelling techniques.

A diorama can help determine the clearances needed on a double track main line where it enters a sharp curve. It also allows you to work out what scenery materials are in proportion for the scale and which appear over-size. It might be that the building of a diorama may help you decide that 'N' gauge modelling is not necessarily right for you – before you have committed yourself too far!

The N Gauge Society is an invaluable resource for all 'N' gauge modellers regardless of experience. Founded in 1967, the society has a huge amount of information in a knowledge database to assist newcomers. It also has a members' help line and a members' shop for a variety of exclusive society products including kits and ready-to-run items. More information can be found on the society's web site at *www.ngaugesociety.com*.

And finally

This short article can only offer a brief overview of 'N' gauge modelling and a taste of what is possible with the scale. Layout design, concepts, control systems and construction are subjects for another time. It is worth looking at back-issues of *Hornby Magazine* for articles covering 'N' gauge subjects and to read the Wheal Annah layout features and those within this Yearbook on West Riding Power – *Hornby Magazine's* latest 'N' gauge project.

Scenery, wiring and baseboard construction techniques are generic modelling techniques which can be applied to 'N' gauge layout construction. Look for those books and magazine articles that offer information on layout construction and wiring and adapt the techniques to suit. Whatever you do, have fun building your railway empire, no matter how small it is! ■

---

7 REASONS TO MODEL IN 'N' GAUGE

1 Less space: Modellers in 'N' have a better chance of finding a small corner for a layout with sufficient operating potential to satisfy the most demanding enthusiast. Storing a sizeable 'N' gauge fleet will also be less demanding than finding storage for larger scale models.

2 More railway in a space: The smaller size of 'N' gauge means you can fit a great deal more railway and operating interest in a given area. A main line railway can be built in a space as small as that normally required for a simple fiddle yard to station branch line in 'OO'.

3 Narrower baseboards: To achieve the same depth of scene in 'N' gauge, baseboards do not need to be as wide as in larger scales. Perfectly believable scenes can be achieved in a 12in deep baseboard.

4 Portability: Moving a layout is no small undertaking and modelling in 'N' gauge may prove to be more practical in this regard by taking advantage of the smaller space and lighter construction needed.

5 Train length: The smaller the scale, the longer the trains you can design into the layout concept meaning you can run longer and more accurate trains.

6 Tighter curves: Most 'N' gauge models can operate on curves as tight as 9in radius compared with minimum radii 20 to 24in for 'OO' gauge – meaning you can fit much more railway into a given space.

7 Greater visual impact: There is no doubt that of all the mainstream scales, 'N' gauge better allows the pursuit of the 'railway in the landscape' approach to railway modelling which may be very attractive to some modellers.

Dapol has produced some beautifully designed models of modern DMUs including the Class 153 and Class 156 together with Mk 3 coaches. They are designed to allow easy removal of the roof to reach an interior lighting plug (light bar) and as seen in this view of the Class 153, the NEM-651 DCC socket.

POWER AND CONTROL

The project layout takes a big step forward with track laying, power connection and point motors. **MIKE WILD** explains how it was done.

EVERY LAYOUT no matter how big or small needs power – and it needs to run reliably if it is going to be enjoyable. Having completed the planning and baseboard construction phases for West Riding Power the project could move forward to become a working railway.

Working in 'N' gauge there are two main choices of track for the British modeller: code 80 and code 55 rail profiles. Code 80 track has a larger rail profile than code 55, but for a change of materials and the desire to represent heavier modern track we selected the code 80 range from Peco as the source of track for West Riding Power. Large radius points have been used throughout the main line.

When it came to powering the new layout there was only one choice and that was for it to follow in the footsteps of previous *Hornby Magazine* layouts by using Digital Command Control (DCC). This system continues to grow in popularity and with more products designed to operate with DCC becoming available it is an ever more viable choice, especially for new layouts.

DCC provides a constant 16v AC supply to the track. Locomotives require a small computer chip called a decoder in order to operate with the system and this interprets signals from the controller to operate the motor, lights and – if fitted - features such as sound as well. This method of control allows much greater flexibility and simplification of wiring. Points and accessories can be operated with the system too, with each item being given its own specific address which allows the controller to communicate with it.

Working in 'N' gauge most new locomotives are now produced with a 6-pin DCC decoder socket installed. Some earlier models aren't factory fitted with a socket including compact engines such as the Class 03, 04 and 08 shunters from the Bachmann

INSTALLING DECODERS IN 'N' GAUGE

A Installing a decoder in a modern 'N' gauge diesel locomotive couldn't be simpler. First the body needs to be removed. The majority of models are a clip fit which require gentle pressure outwards to release the body from the chassis.

B Having removed the body the DCC decoder socket is easily identified. All current models, which are DCC ready, have a 6-pin socket with Graham Farish models having ample space for a Bachmann 36-558A decoder. Dapol models will require a Gaugemaster DCC23 decoder or the equivalent size decoder from an alternative source.

C The final step is to replace the blanking plug with a decoder. Ensure that pin 1 of the decoder aligns with pin 1 on the socket – both are marked – and your locomotive is ready for testing and addressing.

A Class 47 leads an express across the newly built truss bridge. In the background a pair of Class 20s pass through the power station.

Graham Farish stable. However, main line steam and diesel locomotives from Bachmann and Dapol are all fitted with the necessary means to convert them.

Installing decoders in 'N' gauge models is very simple where a decoder socket is provided – you just need to be sure that the decoder you have selected will fit. Bachmann's range is designed to work with its own 6-pin decoder, but decoders from DCC Concepts, Gaugemaster, Lenz and others will work equally well. Dapol's models on the other hand tend to have limited space available for a decoder meaning that careful selection is required to make sure it will fit. Our choices are to use the Bachmann and DCC Concepts 6-pin decoders in Graham Farish locomotives and Gaugemaster DCC23 6-pin decoders in Dapol models.

Track laying

Before trains can start running the track needs to be laid. Throughout the build code 80 flexible track, supplied in yard lengths, has been used with a total of 25yards required to build the entire layout. Allied to this the main line uses large radius straight and curved points throughout – the latter being particularly useful in saving space in the fiddle yard to ensure each road is as long as possible. The only place where medium radius points have been used is for the sidings in the power station.

All points are live frog which offer much better running characteristics as there is no plastic dead section at their centre. Using live frog points does mean considering their installation more carefully as if they are incorrectly installed it can cause electrical shorts. This is most likely to occur in a loop situation with a live frog point at each end. Power has to be fed from the single line end of each point so to stop a conflict in power insulated rail joiners need to be positioned on both rails part way down each loop. This is shown in Diagram 1.

Code 80 'N' gauge flexible track is much easier to work with than the finer profile code 55 – it has greater flexibility as the rail isn't so deeply recessed into the sleeper base - but it does »

WEST RIDING POWER

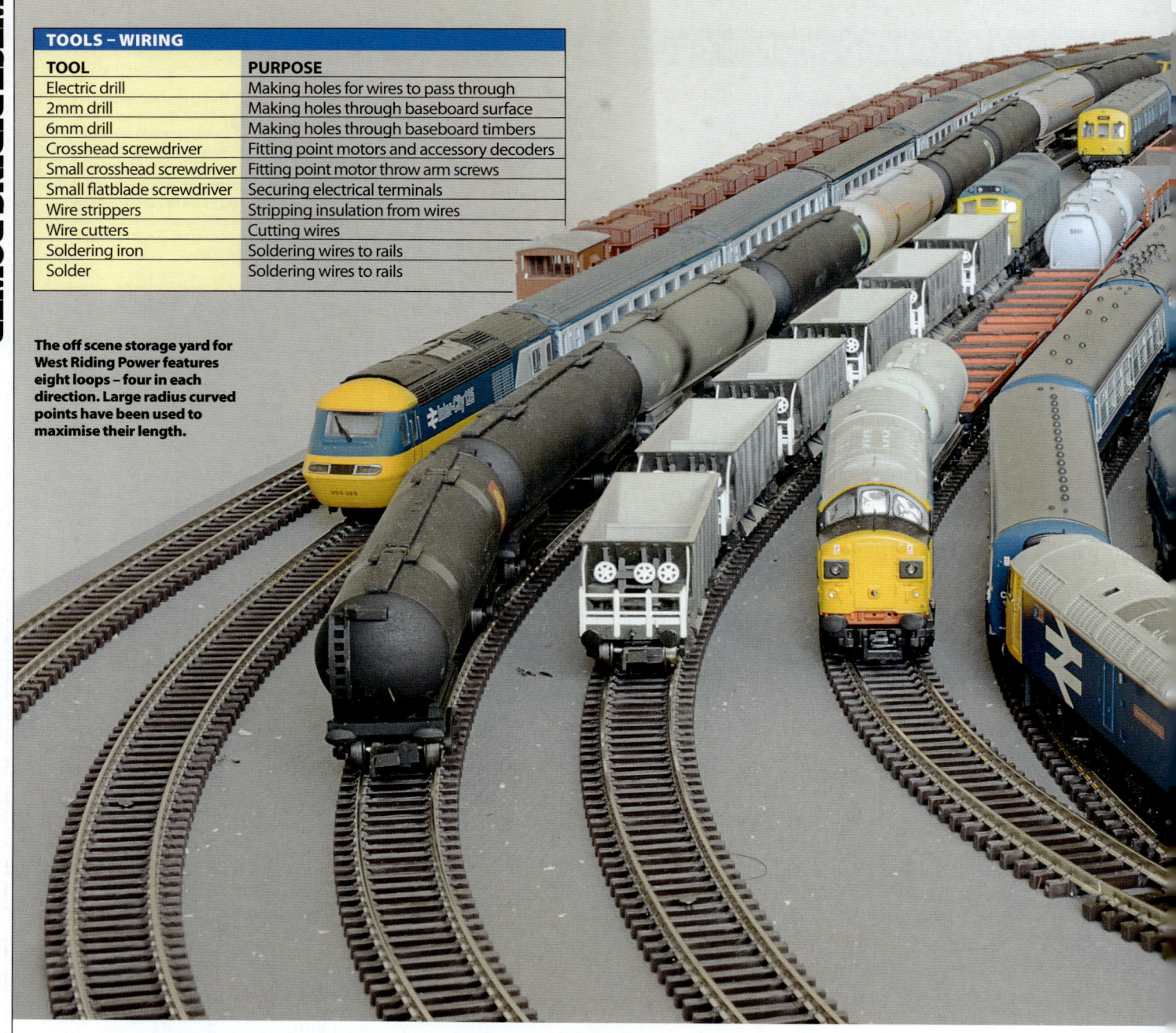

HORNBY MAGAZINE **YEARBOOK 8**

TOOLS – WIRING

TOOL	PURPOSE
Electric drill	Making holes for wires to pass through
2mm drill	Making holes through baseboard surface
6mm drill	Making holes through baseboard timbers
Crosshead screwdriver	Fitting point motors and accessory decoders
Small crosshead screwdriver	Fitting point motor throw arm screws
Small flatblade screwdriver	Securing electrical terminals
Wire strippers	Stripping insulation from wires
Wire cutters	Cutting wires
Soldering iron	Soldering wires to rails
Solder	Soldering wires to rails

The off scene storage yard for West Riding Power features eight loops – four in each direction. Large radius curved points have been used to maximise their length.

LAYING THE TRACK, BUILDING BRIDGES AND INSTALLING POINT MOTORS

1 Track laying revolved around the position of junctions and the bridge at the front of the layout. Code 80 track has been used throughout with a combination of flexible track and large radius straight and curved points.

2 Large radius curved points have been used to create the storage yard approaches. Peco ST-280 track pins have been used to fix the track in place.

Diagram 1 - Wiring

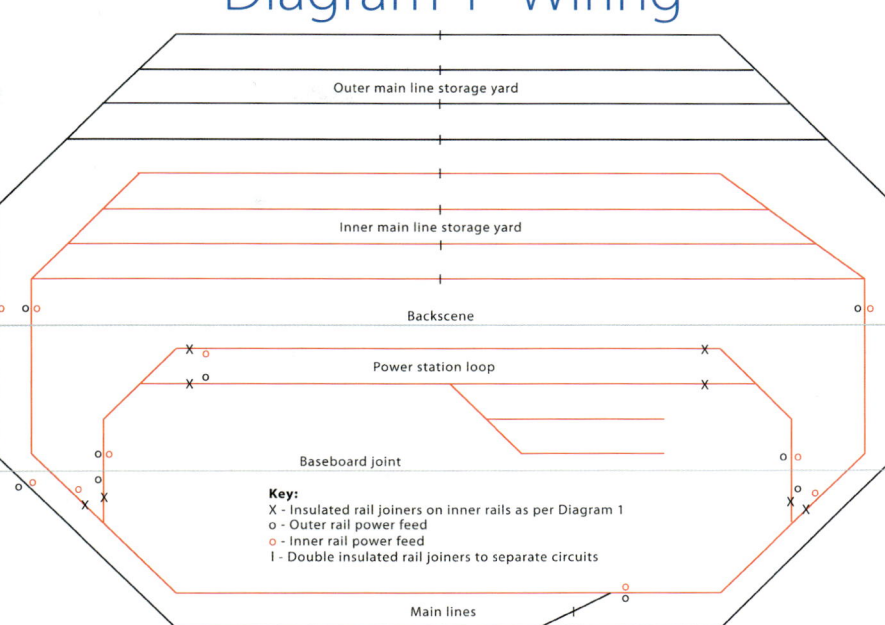

Outer main line storage yard

Inner main line storage yard

Backscene

Power station loop

Baseboard joint

Key:
X - Insulated rail joiners on inner rails as per Diagram 1
o - Outer rail power feed
o - Inner rail power feed
I - Double insulated rail joiners to separate circuits

Main lines

still require separate rail joiners to join lengths together. Rail joiners also need to be fitted to all points from the code 80 Streamline range.

To join the track metal and plastic rail joiners have been used. The latter have been positioned on the inner rail ends of each point so that the whole scenic section can be kept live at all times meaning that even with a point set against a train its lights will remain on – see Diagram 2. This also increases operational potential as, for example, a train can continue crawling through the power station unloading shed while a main line train overtakes without the freight train having to stop.

Track is pinned direct to the baseboard surface using Peco's larger diameter ST-280 track pins. While these are more obtrusive visually than the finer pins, they are much more robust and easier to use. They require a 1mm hole to be drilled through the sleeper before being inserted using a hand worked pin vice. The finer pins are very easily bent meaning a high wastage figure. To ensure the hammer doesn't contact the track during pinning a pin punch was used.

While the majority of the track laying on West Riding Power is very simple, there is one major feature which took more construction – the truss frame bridge at the front centre of the scenic section. We wanted this to feature a see-through frame below the running rails, as per the prototype, with walkways on each side and brick supports.

To do this Evergreen plastic strip was used to create four longitudinal beams for the running rails which were then glued to 'I' section girders using Deluxe Materials plastic cement. Walkways were added on each side, 8mm wide, using 1mm thick plasticard and further detail was added by using square section to create bracing underneath the track. To complete the framework of the bridge Peco truss bridge sides were added and the whole assembly was painted with Railmatch roof dirt colour from an aerosol. »

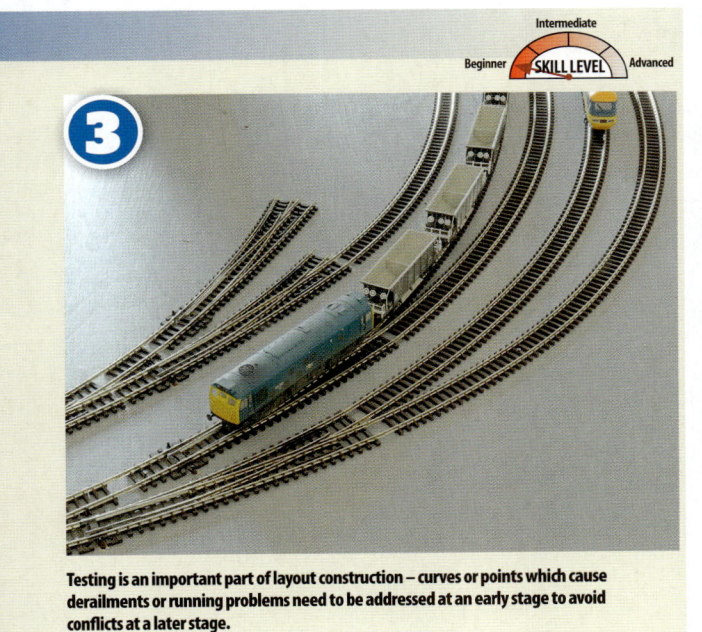

3 Testing is an important part of layout construction – curves or points which cause derailments or running problems need to be addressed at an early stage to avoid conflicts at a later stage.

SKILL LEVEL: Beginner / Intermediate / Advanced

WHAT WE USED

PRODUCT	MANUFACTURER	CAT NO.
Code 80 flexible track, yard lengths	Peco	SL300
Code 80 large radius right point	Peco	SL-E388
Code 80 large radius left point	Peco	SL-E389
Code 80 large radius curved right point	Peco	SL-E386
Code 80 large radius curved left point	Peco	SL-E387
Code 80 medium radius right point	Peco	SL-E395
Code 80 medium radius left point	Peco	SL-E396
'N' gauge rail joiners, metal	Peco	SL-310
'N' gauge rail joiners, plastic (insulated)	Peco	SL-311
Additional wooden sleepers	Peco	SL-308F
Large track pins	Peco	ST-280
Cobalt IP digital point motors	DCC Concepts	DCP-CB12DIP
7/0.2 equipment wire, orange	Rapid Electronics	01-0425
7/0.2 equipment wire, green	Rapid Electronics	01-0415
Plug-in terminal block, white (Hylec)	Rapid Electronics	21-4278
Square section plastic strip 2.5mm x 2.5mm	Evergreen	175
'I' section plastic strip, 4.8mm	Evergreen	276
1mm thick plasticard	Evergreen	9040
Two aspect starter colour light signal	Eckon	BN02
Three aspect colour light signal	Eckon	BN38
Two aspect colour light signal decoder	Train-Tech	SC1
Three aspect colour light signal decoder	Train-Tech	SC2

WEST RIDING POWER

www.hornbymagazine.com

Wanting the track to the look the part the sleepers were removed from the flexible track for the full length of the bridge and then carefully glued to the new plastic supports – set at the correct gauge. The gauge of the rails was checked during setting of the glue to ensure that trains would run smoothly across the new bridge.

Power

To provide the power for the layout a selection of digital control systems is available. West Riding Power has a choice of three systems for operation: the Gaugemaster Prodigy system, Hornby's RailMaster computer control system and Bachmann's recently released Dynamis Ultima. All three offer an ample 4amp supply for controlling 'N' gauge locomotives and the low current draw accessories which will be installed.

A main power connection has been created on the layout at one corner of the storage yard allowing a controller base station to be plugged in using our preferred method of a plug-in terminal block – this allows controllers to be moved from one layout to another simply by disconnecting the two pin plug.

From here power is distributed through a main power bus made from 16 strand cable to a second plug in terminal block. This is used as a distribution point to provide power to track sections, the jumper cable between the baseboards and the accessory modules. From here the wiring is with seven strand equipment wire which carries power to sections of the layout.

The whole of the scenic section is live meaning that trains can be driven whether points are set against them or not. In the storage yard power connection to each track is handled by the points to simplify wiring. To make the scenic section live requires insulated rail joiners to be added to the middle two rails at the toe end of the point – the outer rails being fitted with metal rail joiners for conductivity. To power the inner isolated rails beyond the point a single wire is soldered to the corresponding rail and then linked back to the distribution point to provide power to the section. Diagram 2 shows the electrical set up for the layout.

This is the third time that we have used this arrangement for delivering DCC power to our layouts following great success with both Twelve Trees Junction (Yearbook No. 6) and Shortley Bridge and Felton Cement Works (Yearbook No. 7). It is particularly helpful where locomotives are fitted with lights and sound on DCC as these features can remain on even when a point is set against them mimicking the real railway more accurately. »

Diagram 2 - Riding Power wiring

The power station loop features four points to provide two tracks through the discharge shed and also for a pair of sidings. A Class 56 moves through the discharge shed at the head of a rake of HAA hoppers.

LAYING THE TRACK, BUILDING BRIDGES AND INSTALLING POINT MOTORS

SKILL LEVEL: Intermediate

4 Dropper wires were soldered to the rail sides in positions where they would be least visible using 7/0.2 equipment wire. A Class 37 leads a rake of Presflos round one of the corners from the storage yard during testing of the electrics.

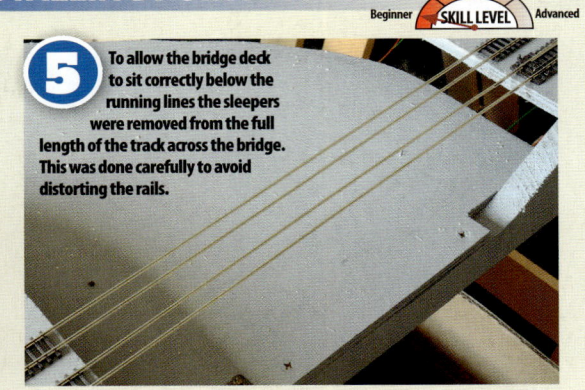

5 To allow the bridge deck to sit correctly below the running lines the sleepers were removed from the full length of the track across the bridge. This was done carefully to avoid distorting the rails.

6 The truss bridge at the centre front of the layout features a base made up from Evergreen plastic strip. 2.5mm square section has been used for the longitudinal beams under the running rails with 5mm 'I' section for the supporting frame work. The walkways on each side are cut 8mm wide from 1mm thick plasticard.

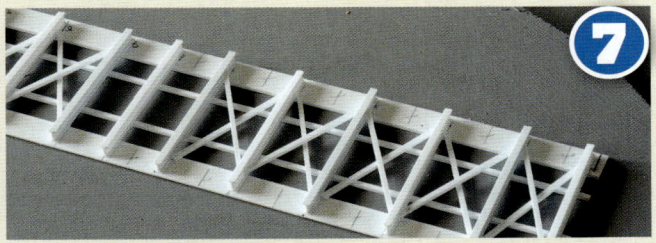

7 To further detail the underside and provide a suggestion of strength cross braces were added between each 'I' beam using 2.5mm square section. The entire bridge was glued together using Deluxe Materials Plastic Magic supplied by Gaugemaster.

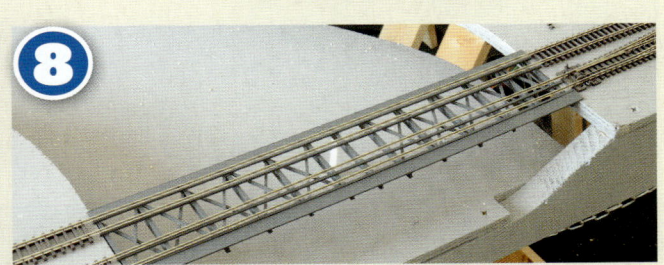

8 The completed bridge deck was painted with RailMatch Roof Dirt from an aerosol spray can with the truss sides being painted separately at the same time.

9 To fix the rails to the bridge deck impact adhesive was used for a strong joint. The drying time also allows for small adjustments to be made once the bridge deck was fitted to the rails.

10 With the bridge sides fitted, again using contact adhesive, test running proved the strength of the bridge deck with a single support – during the scenic development structural supports will be built for the bridge from plasticard.

TOOLS – TRACK LAYING

TOOL	PURPOSE
Pin hammer	Tapping track pins home
Pin punch	To keep the hammer away from track when adding pins
Pliers	Manipulating track into position
Minidrill and cutting disc	Cutting track to length
Pin vice	Drilling 1mm holes in sleepers to accept track pins
1mm drill bit	Drilling 1mm holes in sleepers to accept track pins

WEST RIDING POWER

LAYING THE TRACK, BUILDING BRIDGES AND INSTALLING POINT MOTORS

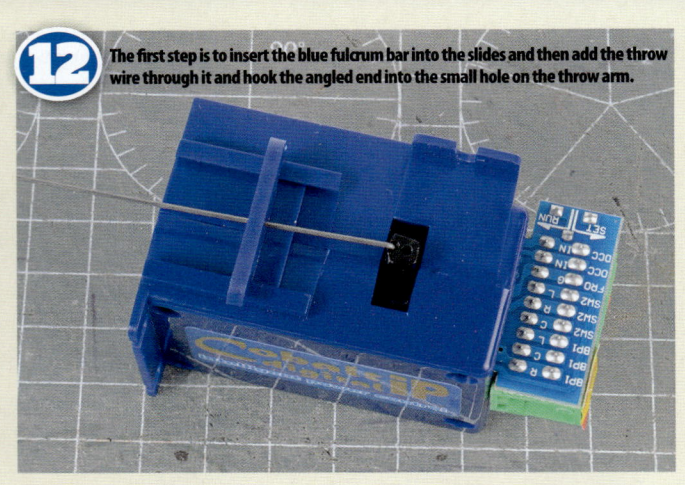

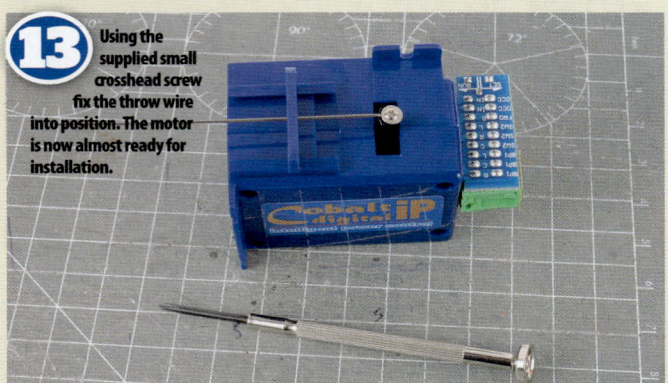

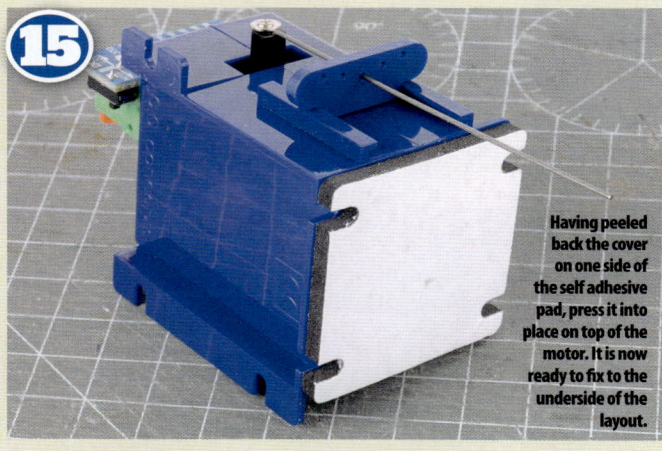

11 The point motors on West Riding Power are DCC Concepts Cobalt IP digital motors – these are factory fitted with a DCC decoder making them very simple and quick to install.

12 The first step is to insert the blue fulcrum bar into the slides and then add the throw wire through it and hook the angled end into the small hole on the throw arm.

13 Using the supplied small crosshead screw fix the throw wire into position. The motor is now almost ready for installation.

14 A very useful feature of the fitting kit supplied with the Cobalt IP digital motors are these self adhesive pads – they make installation a doddle!

15 Having peeled back the cover on one side of the self adhesive pad, press it into place on top of the motor. It is now ready to fix to the underside of the layout.

16 The Cobalt IP digital motors have a built in DCC accessory decoder which is addressed through the learn button next to the contacts. Here it is set in run mode…

17 …by moving the switch down into set mode the point motor can be addressed simply by selecting the accessory address you want it to be on a digital handset and changing it. This mode is also used for DCC Concepts special functions to change the direction of the motor (enter address 197) and to turn off the self-centring function (enter address 198). Once programming is complete return the switch back to run mode.

18 With the backing paper removed from the top side of the self-adhesive pad the throw arm can be directed through a hole in the baseboard and through the hole on the tie bar of the point above. The throw arm will need cutting to length after installation. Ensure the point is in the correct position at the time of fitting so that on changing the motor will pull the point across.

19 With the digital Cobalt motors wiring couldn't be simpler – each motor can be 'daisy chained' to the next using 7/0.2 equipment wire as each motor has a low current draw. Simply pull the tag up and insert the DCC bus wires into the correct holes.

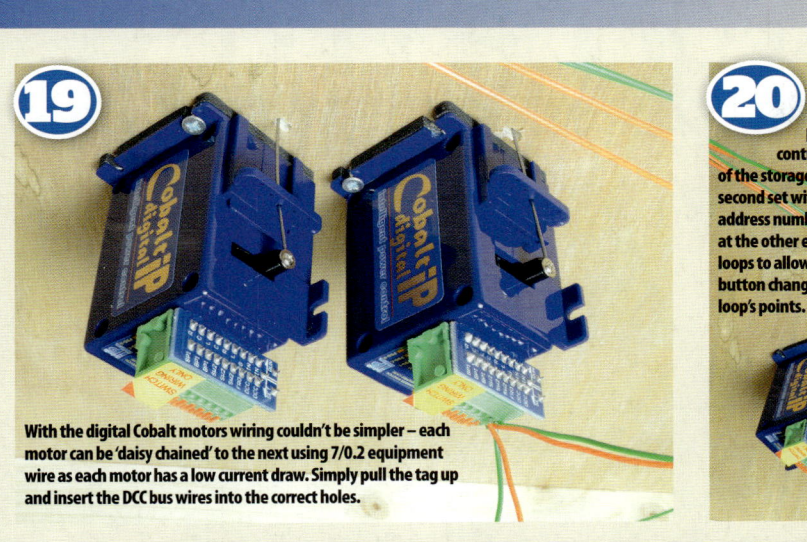

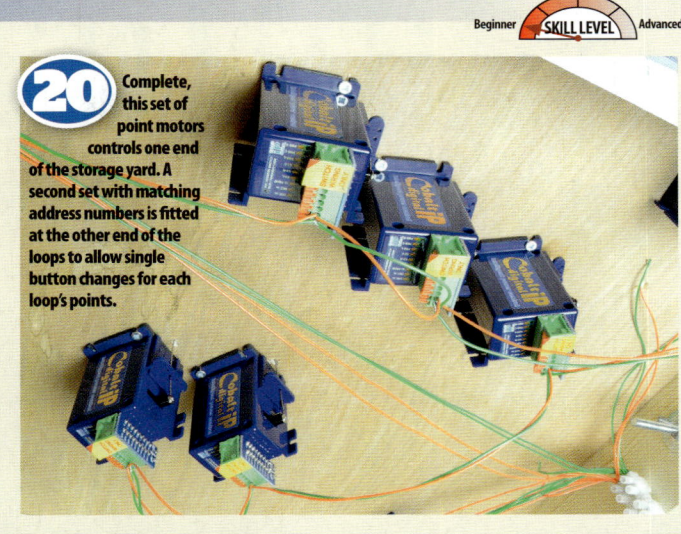

20 Complete, this set of point motors controls one end of the storage yard. A second set with matching address numbers is fitted at the other end of the loops to allow single button changes for each loop's points.

Accessories

Completing the electrical line up on West Riding Power are point motors and colour light signals. Point motors are DCC Concepts Cobalt motors which we have found to be reliable in service and very quick and simple to install. All of the points have been kitted out with Digital Cobalt IP motors which are delivered with a DCC accessory decoder pre-installed. These are very quick to install with all 24 motors on the layout being installed, wired and addressed within two hours.

The DCC Concepts DCC fitted Cobalts all offer three optional settings and come factory set to return to centre when power is started up on the DCC system. Turning this feature off is simple requiring all motors to be switched into programming mode and address 198 to be entered. This turns off the self centring which can be turned back on using the same procedure and entering address 199. The third special function is achieved using address 197 – this switches the polarity of the accessory decoder in each case. We used this function for setting up the left hand end of the storage yard and it means that points are thrown in pairs, by giving points at each end of a loop the same address, so that only one accessory address needs to be selected to allow the next train to depart. The DCC Concepts point motor products also allow for a feedback control panel to be built. This will form a future project for West Riding Power in the pages of *Hornby Magazine*.

The final element on the electrical front are four colour light signals from the Eckon range supplied by Gaugemaster. These pre-assembled colour lights are very simple to install and require a single 3mm diameter hole to be drilled through the baseboard underneath their base to allow the connecting wires to pass through. The wiring of the signals is colour coded – green for green, red for red, yellow for yellow – with a resistor being fitted on the negative lead to control voltage to the lights.

To make installation simple and avoid the need for a separate power supply, we used Train-Tech colour light signal decoders (also supplied by Gaugemaster) to connect the signals to the DCC control network on West Riding Power. These provide for both common positive and common negative wiring with the Eckon signals requiring the wire with the resistor to be connected to the negative connection on the decoder. The coloured wires from the signal are then connected in turn to the outputs (numbered 1-4 on both the two aspect and three/four aspect accessory decoders by Train-Tech) making them ready to programme with addresses. The latter stage is taken care of by using the learn button – once pressed the signal will flash and by selecting the address on a DCC handset and changing it the address of the decoder is established.

With all this done West Riding Power is ready to move onto the next stage of work – detailing of the scenery to make the bare baseboards represent the real world around a power station. Turn to pages 78-85 to read about the scenic construction of the layout. ■

An HST set speeds across the truss bridge as a pair of Class 20s enters the power station loop. By this stage the layout is ready for the start of scenic work.

LAYOUT MAINTENANCE

Keeping trains moving

A smooth running railway is an enjoyable model. **NIGEL BURKIN** reveals his top tips to get the best performance from ready-to-run locomotives and rolling stock.

When the time comes for a layout operating session you want everything to run as smoothly as possible without derailments, stalling or jerky running. Keeping the layout in tip-top condition requires maintenance and periodic checks to see that track, turnouts, wiring, controls and locomotives are all working satisfactorily.

A great deal of cleaning work to track, structures and scenery can be prevented by using dust sheets to cover the layout between running sessions. The best material for protecting the layout from dust is the lightweight plastic sheet sold by DIY retailers. It is light enough to avoid damaging delicate structures and scenery and will not pull rolling stock off the layout during removal.

LAYOUT MAINTENANCE

THERE IS NOTHING MORE frustrating than a poorly running layout. Derailments, jerky running and stalling on points will make any modeller ask if the investment in wood, track, wiring, control system and scenery – and above all, effort - was really worth it. Problems inevitably arise because model railways are complex animals made of a number of different and sometimes incompatible materials.

It does not have to be that way – maintenance and making small but effective improvements can bring many benefits to a less than reliable layout. Here we will look at some of the causes of poor performance, how they can be avoided and how to maintain a model railway so it runs well.

The design stage

When starting a model railway you have the opportunity to design your layout for reliability as well as realism. One thing I have learned not to do is skimp on quality materials or apply small but ultimately meaningless economies. Experienced modellers will use dowels on portable layouts for accurate baseboard alignment every time the layout is assembled. They are worth every penny!

The box of recovered telephony wire under one of the layouts at the club will not provide reliable electrical supply in the long term. Spend some of your budget on quality equipment wire, no matter if it is a Digital Command Control (DCC) or analogue layout. Use 7/0.2mm grade for accessories and a heavier grade of wire such as 16/0.2mm is perfect for most analogue control applications. DCC control will require wire capable of carrying up to 5amps for some distance without voltage drop, so choose a grade as beefy as 24/0.2mm. That way, you will avoid voltage drop and wiring faults!

Timber for baseboards is another key choice which can make or break a layout. Heavier baseboard design will be more durable, so do not hesitate to upgrade from 9mm to 12mm plywood for box frames and baseboard tops for »

LAYOUT MAINTENANCE

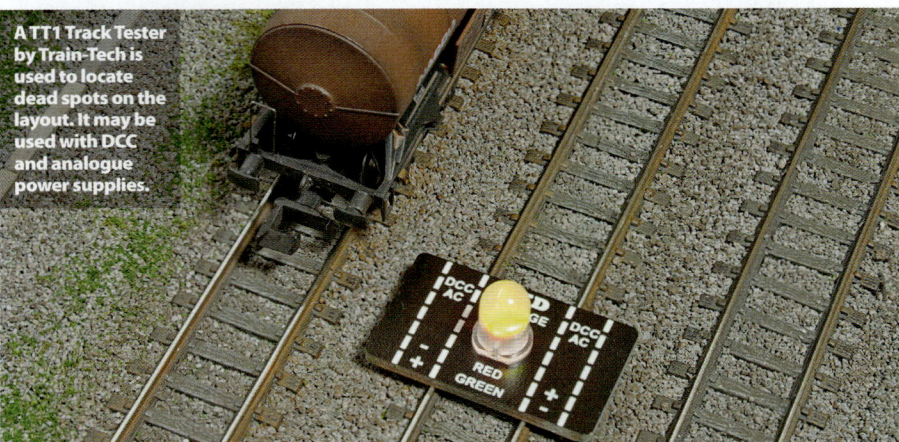

Use a brush to sweep dust, fragments of scenery and pet hairs from buildings where it looks very unsightly. The same soft brush can be used to clean out the flange ways of turnouts and common crossings. Look for stray ballast and pieces of scenery in points which can cause a derailment and prevent points from operating smoothly.

A TT1 Track Tester by Train-Tech is used to locate dead spots on the layout. It may be used with DCC and analogue power supplies.

Once the rails are clean, some modellers choose to condition them to prevent arcing and tarnish build-up, reducing the frequency of cleaning sessions. A popular product is Rail-Zip2 which is applied and left to dry overnight.

A gentle rub with a soft track rubber will remove most, if not all of the grime build-up from the rails. The idea is to burnish the rails gently, not abrade them!

Potential trouble spots can include turnout points that fail to throw properly (A); track details such as conductor rail which has become dislodged or raised (B); track side structures that are out of gauge and catch passing trains (C); tight clearances in common crossings (D); misaligned rail joiners (E) and damaged point blades (F).

the sake of an extra kilo or so in weight. If the layout is not intended to be transported on a regular basis, consider using 18mm plywood for maximum stability - the additional cost will repay you many times over. Choose plywood which has a good number of layers making up its structure and has no joins or knots to ensure the stability of your baseboards.

When drawing up a track plan, have you given any consideration as to its accessibility? Will there be any hidden track? How accessible will it be? Consider how derailed stock will be recovered without damage; track cleaned and wiring repaired in those areas.

Avoid excessively sharp curves and test your longest items of rolling stock for clearances to determine the spacing between tracks on curves. When venturing into track laying, be sure your baseboard top is flat and no screws protrude above the surface. Buy a countersink bit to make recesses for screw heads during construction. Lay your points so they are flat and avoid placing them at the bottom or top of an incline to avoid derailments at the change in gradient. Leave a small gap at each rail joint to allow for summer expansion unless you are track laying on a particularly hot day, which should be avoided.

Consider how rail ends will be secured at the baseboard ends of portable layouts so they will be safe from damage during transportation and

LAYOUT MAINTENANCE

storage. They must align with the adjacent rails of the next baseboard every time without having to be adjusted! The owners of fixed layouts will not need to consider baseboard joints.

Bigger isn't always better

Owning a large fleet of models on a large layout might seem like the ultimate dream of most railway modellers. Assuming you have both time and resources to complete the layout, maintenance will also be an issue. How long will it take to clean track, wheels, pick-ups and undertake routine maintenance checks to keep the layout running well?

For example, my North American 'N' scale layout occupies a 400 square foot room on two levels linked with a helix. The main line run is nearly 220ft in length excluding loops and sidings. That is a lot of track to keep clean! The fleet consists of 340 bogie freight wagons; and each one has two couplers, four axles and eight wheels. That is 680 couplers to check and over 2,700 wheels to clean from time to time. When the layout is complete, the fleet will consist of around 450 wagons and the only way I will be able to keep track of them will be to have a simple maintenance programme.

In contrast, my latest 'OO' gauge project for *Hornby Magazine* is a compact layout based on the Speyside line in the mid 1960s. It will run with

The art of keeping the track (actually the rails) clean of grime, oil, dust and tarnish has resulted in a wide variety of products from simple abrasive rubbers, specialised solutions and increasingly sophisticated track cleaning vehicles.

two Bo-Bo locomotives together with an Andrew Barclay 0-4-0ST totalling 18 wheels. It will have a maximum track length including fiddle yard and sidings of just 25ft and no more than about 15 two axle wagons. Clearly, the maintenance »

RUNNING SESSION CHECK LIST

Preparing for a running session will make a big difference to a layout's performance and your enjoyment of a layout. Here's a ten point check list which applies to fixed as well as portable layouts:

● Remove the dust covers carefully and power up the layout to find obvious electrical faults.

● If all is well, clean and condition the rails and vacuum the track.

● Test the models. Clean wheels and check current collection pick-ups if performance is not up to scratch.

● Test the points and signals.

● Check that batteries for wireless controllers are fully charged and spares are available.

● Look for dust and dirt on the layout, locomotives and stock and clean it away.

● Look for and remove any tools and materials left behind from repair and fine tuning sessions.

● Run a handful of trains to test the layout and look for any new problems that might have arisen and in time to repair them.

● Check any baseboard joints for misalignment and adjust where necessary.

● Touch in and repair any dints or scratches to the fascia and pelmets.

LAYOUT MAINTENANCE

A little effort put into layout maintenance and cleaning will bring a lot of rewards in improving running of your trains and a better-looking layout. A 20ton brake van equipped with a roller cleaning attachment is hauled by a Bachmann Class 20 – the brake van can be run in a regular freight train and gently cleans the track while it runs around the layout.

TEN WAYS OF IMPROVING AND

There are many things you can do to keep the layout running reliably all the time. A couple of hours of and parcel of your railway modelling routine – you have spent a considerable amount of time and

1 Clean the track

Track and rail cleaning is an essential task which is needed to remove the build up of grime resulting from dust, lubricant, tarnish and arcing. Almost every modeller has a different solution for keeping the rails clean to maximise electrical conductivity and naturally, the condition in which the layout is kept and run will have a big impact on the causes of track dirt.

The simplest way to clean the rails is to use a gentle track rubber such as the one offered by C&L Finescale. Avoid abrading the rail head – the action has to be hard enough to remove stubborn dirt but not so harsh as to grind the rails. Track cleaning fluid rubbed along the rails with a soft cloth also works.

There are also mechanical track cleaners such as that offered by Dapol or chemical track cleaners such as the CMX tank wagon which is filled with track cleaning fluid. Finally, if you have recently completed work on a layout, run a magnet along the track to collect ferrous items such as track pins and off-cuts of point motor throw bars before locomotive motors do.

Once the track has been cleaned there is the option of conditioning the rails to reduce the impact of arcing and tarnish. A popular conditioning product is RailZip2 which is applied to the track with a soft cloth and left to dry overnight.

2 Inspect points and crossings

It pays to inspect each point and test the mechanism to be sure that the blades are locking correctly. The slightest gap between the stock rail and point blade will catch wheel flanges and tip a train off the track or cause the train to 'split the points'.

Another source of poor running are the electrical contacts of some off-the-shelf turnouts including Hornby, Peco and Bachmann track systems. For example, Peco Streamline 'OO' gauge points rely on tabs to make the electrical contact between the point blade and stock rail to power the turnout. Eventually, these tabs may become worn, dirty or break completely which causes a dead section in the turnout. Peco 'N' gauge turnouts rely on the spring locking of the points to make the same electrical contact which is not that reliable after a while. All versions of Peco 'N' and 'OO' gauge turnouts can be modified to overcome this fault by electrically bonding the switch and stock rails together at the build stage.

3 Investigate persistent derailments

There is a simple way of checking the cause of a derailment. If trains persistently derail in the same place, it is likely that the track is at fault. An inspection is what is required to find the cause – solder, dirt, physical damage or even something fouling the track may be the cause. If a particular wagon or coach derails persistently, but at random places on the layout, it is more likely that the fault is with the rolling stock, not the track. Check the wheels with an accurate back to back gauge and adjust where necessary – incorrect back to back settings, the distance between the inner faces of the wheels, are the main cause of derailments. Other potential causes can include misaligned couplings, a twisted bogie, unseated wheel set or an out-of-true underframe.

4 Test the track for gauge

One set of tools all railway modellers should own are track gauges. They consist of rail gauge and flangeway clearance gauges. Either conduct spot checks of your track using gauges to look for misalignment or use the gauges to test known trouble spots. Run a

An example of roller gauges for testing the gauge of track and the correct flangeway clearance on turnouts. Gauges such as these will soon tell you why your trains are derailing consistently at a particular location.

demands of the compact layout are considerably less onerous and would better suit someone with a hectic lifestyle. After all, spending more than an hour or two doing maintenance before being able to play trains is no fun. That said, there are things that can be done to reduce maintenance and cleaning to leave more time for running trains!

Look for trouble

It pays to look for trouble on your layout from time to time. Do some inspections of the layout to identify trouble spots. When you dropped those pliers during a building session, did they kink a running rail? What happened to that stray spot of scenery paint?

Looking over the layout for physical damage, gently tweaking the wiring to see that it is secure, running your finger over rail joints to check for burrs and misalignment, operating turnouts to see that they are not sticking and looking for details that have fallen off models is an inspection routine which will pick out trouble spots before you invite your friends over for an operating session. Removing burrs and checking turnout point blades for rough edges and removing them is simple tweaking which makes a layout run better.

Maintenance, while perhaps appearing onerous on the surface, becomes a matter of course and while there are times when it might seem like a chore turning your attention to cleaning the rails and wheels and locomotives alone will result in a much smoother running layout. And, ultimately, a smooth running layout is an enjoyable one to operate too. ■

MAINTAINING YOUR LAYOUT...

fine tuning can deliver a massive improvement in the way the trains run. Make the following part money building your railway, so it would be a shame not to get the best out of it.

short train of reliable stock over the layout and observe it closely – you are looking for tight spots or places where the wheels ride onto the running rail, even briefly. Check these places with track gauges to find the cause of the trouble.

5 Look for expansion problems

Failing to leave a small gap of around 1mm to 1.5mm at rail joins when tracklaying may result in expansion problems when the layout room becomes hot in summer. If the rails expand and lift or buckle the track, it can be seated back into place by cutting the rails part way along the affected section using a cutting disc or Xuron track cutters in-situ. Do not forget to clean any burrs from the cuts and be prepared to solder additional feeds to the track.

6 Examine the wiring

It does not hurt to look over the layout's wiring from time to time to see that the wiring is secure and nothing has come adrift since the layout was last moved, especially for portable layouts. There is always the chance of a dry solder joint which results in a poor connection between the rails and the layout's wiring, so check the connections between the wiring and track. Avoid hanging wiring because you can guarantee that it will snag something and be pulled off.

7 Lubricate moving parts

The key moving parts on the operational side of a model railway will be the points of turnouts and the associated mechanism. Avoid using oil on turnout stretcher bar assemblies – a trace of dry lubricant such as graphite puffed into the mechanism is far better! Other moving parts needing cleaning and lubrication include signal mechanisms and turntables; all of which must move slowly and smoothly. A very light model oil which is 'plastic safe' should be applied very sparingly to moving parts and the excess wiped off.

8 Protect from dust and dirt

How many layout owners cover their layouts when they are not in use? Dust and other domestic dirt such as pet hairs will spoil the presentation of a layout and takes ages to clean from the top of locomotives and rolling stock. Whilst a layout can be brushed and vacuumed gently to remove dust, there is always the risk of damaging delicate structures and vacuuming up scenery and details! Plastic dust sheets sold in DIY shops as decorating drop cloths are perfect as dust covers. Portable layouts can be equipped with hard covers to protect the layout during transportation.

9 Check the layout for damage

A great way of looking for damage to scenery and structures, not to mention parts lost from locomotives and rolling stock, is to photograph the layout. It is amazing what you will see in a picture that the eye misses when looking over the layout.

10 How presentable is the layout?

Once again, your eye could miss details that become apparent in photographs, so consider using photography as a tool for looking at your layout from a different angle. You are looking for damage or marks in the presentational side of the layout, particularly those that are exhibited or occupy living space in the home and need to look presentable.

GALLERY

HORNBY MAGAZINE YEARBOOK 8

Master
in the Gallery

Created by Bob Hunter and modelled in Gauge 1, Hatherleigh Junction might not have featured an amazing array of pointwork, but the beautiful modelling of scenic features and the locomotives and rolling stock more than made up for that. It represents a section of the line in North Devon bringing Western Region diesel hydraulics and Southern Region steam side by side. Bulleid 'West Country' 34019 *Bideford* – an Aster model – enters the station from the off-scene storage yard. Hatherleigh Junction featured in HM98.

Trevor Jones/Hornby Magazine.

pieces

Model railways cover a spectrum of interests and styles. *Hornby Magazine's* Editor **MIKE WILD** brings together a collection of images highlighting some of the favourites featured in the magazine over the past 12 months.

GALLERY

Dainton Bank (above)

Michael Heaven's Dainton Bank bowed out from the exhibition circuit at the end of 2014 having been taken on as a memorial to him by the 82G Group. The final show for this monster 50ft long 'O' gauge layout was the Warley National Model Railway Exhibition in November 2014. On a balmy summer Saturday a Collett 'Castle' crests the gradient and passes Dainton Tunnel signalbox while a '57XX' 0-6-0PT and a '51XX' 2-6-2T simmer in the siding having banked a train up the gradient. Dainton Bank featured in HM92. *Mike Wild/Hornby Magazine.*

Retford

Roy Jackson's model of Retford in 'EM' gauge is famed throughout British modelling circles not least for the fact that this scale model, which includes the flat crossing between the Great Northern and Great Central routes, measures more than 70ft in length and features the East Coast Main Line's most prestigious trains from 1957. In an element of modelling subterfuge, a BR liveried Gresley 'P2' 2-8-2 – none survived long enough in service to receive this livery – heads north and passes the unique Gresley 'W1' 4-6-4 60700 on the East Coast Main Line while a 'WD' 2-8-0 waits patiently at the signals on the Great Central route for a clear path. Retford featured in HM100. *Mike Wild/Hornby Magazine.*

Penhallick (above)

This exhibition favourite first featured in the pages of *Hornby Magazine* in January 2012 (HM56), but since then it has been retired and rebuilt into a new permanent layout for the owning group of Jerry Winterson, Mel Rees and friends. Representing North Cornwall on the Southern and Western Regions in 4mm scale a Maunsell 'N' 2-6-0 approaches the terminus with an engineers' train as a BR '4MT' 2-6-0 departs from the coastal terminus. Penhallick featured in HM101. Trevor Jones/*Hornby Magazine*.

64 HORNBY MAGAZINE YEARBOOK 8

GALLERY

Bray Down

If ever you thought modelling the Western Region meant a quaint terminus with short trains, Graeme Davies' Bray Down would have changed all that. Featuring a four track main line split into two and three sides of scenery – and with a branch line too – this inspirational 'OO' scale layout featured a mixture of Western and Southern motive power. At Bray Down Junction a Churchward '28XX' 2-8-0 passes a Collett '4575' 2-6-2T at the entrance to Little Parva tunnel as a '57XX' 0-6-0PT emerges on the branch line. Bray Down featured in HM90 and HM91. *Mike Wild/Hornby Magazine.*

Charnwood Forest Branch (Left)

The Soar Valley Model Railway Club realised a 30 year ambition when it completed its 47ft x 13ft model of the Charnwood Forest Branch in 'O' gauge modelling Gracedieu viaduct together with Whitwick and Loughborough Derby Road stations. Featuring entirely scratch built buildings and an awe inspiring footprint this brilliant layout captured the spirit of what working in a club environment can achieve. Stanier 2-6-4T 42430 enters the station at Whitwick to pass a Brush Type 2 rekindling memories of the 1960s railway. The Charnwood Forest Branch featured in HM99 and HM100. *Mike Wild/Hornby Magazine.*

Chillingbourne (Below)

Rural railway operations in Kent are epitomised by Chris White's delightful through station of Chillingbourne. With its collection of pre-grouping locomotive designs and supremely detailed scenic aspect this layout showed the potential of working with a small space and making everything blend together. An 'R1' 0-6-0T simmers in the loop to wait for the arrival of a 'C' 0-6-0 to clear the single line branch. Chillingbourne featured in HM91. *Trevor Jones/Hornby Magazine.*

GALLERY

Dentdale

The Settle and Carlisle line is one of Britain's great railway journeys, and to really model the spectacular drama of its scenery 'N' gauge is the perfect choice. Bob Taylor, Wayne Webb and Tony Frazer did just that in this impressive exhibition layout, Dentdale. Built to be run in the steam era and the modern diesel era too, this impressive 20ft long layout firmly set trains in the landscape. Modelling a steam special a Stanier 'Duchess' 4-6-2 steams away from Dentdale with a Class 67 bringing up the rear of its smartly turned out rake of BR Mk 1 carriages. Dentdale featured in HM95. *Trevor Jones/Hornby Magazine.*

www.hornbymagazine.com 67

GALLERY

Trebudoc

Andy Peter's Cornish branch line terminus proves that you don't need a converted barn to model a realistic setting in 'O' gauge. Occupying just 9ft 6in in length this characterful station boasts all the features you could want with space for both passenger and freight operations. Framed by the road bridge which forms the break between scenery and storage yard, GWR '56XX' 0-6-2T 5637 prepares to depart with a pick up goods. Trebudoc featured in HM96. *Mike Wild/Hornby Magazine.*

Rumbling Bridge

BR's Scottish Region has long been a popular subject amongst modellers and Rumbling Bridge by Nick Skelton is a great example of how it can be done. Built in 'OO' gauge this impressively detailed through station features a mix of steam and diesel traction as well as full Digital Command Control operation and sound in a variety of locomotives. Representing a typical cement working of the 1960s a Class 17 enters the station loop to wait for a path along the single line. Rumbling Bridge featured in HM94. *Mike Wild/Hornby Magazine.*

Haddon Bank

Chelmsford and District Model Railway Club's Haddon Bank recalls the activities on BR's Eastern Region in the 1960s when steam was being joined by the new wave of diesel traction. Modelled in 'OO' gauge this exhibition layout has been a popular feature at shows around the country and continues to be so. A Robinson 'O4' 2-8-0 leads a mineral train over the road and canal as a Cravens DMU descends the gradient on the branch line. Haddon Bank featured in HM91.

Trevor Jones/Hornby Magazine.

Aisthorpe

Lincoln and District Model Railway Society reshaped history with this 'O' gauge exhibition layout which creates a might have been railway in Lincolnshire using the name of their nearby village. A 'C12' 4-4-2T pauses at the station for the arrival of a BR '4MT' 4-6-0 with a mineral train. Aisthorpe featured in HM95.
Mike Wild/Hornby Magazine.

Broadwater Junction

The Warley Model Railway Club's 'N' gauge section is highly active on the exhibition circuit with both British and American layouts, with Broadwater Junction being a stalwart of the scene. A Collett 'Manor' 4-6-0 leads an express through the junction recapturing the early 1960s on BR's Western Region. Broadwater Junction featured in HM89. *Mike Wild/Hornby Magazine.*

Twelve Trees Junction

Two years ago in *Hornby Magazine Yearbook No. 6* the team built a brand new 'OO' gauge exhibition layout set on BR's Southern Region in the 1960s. The result was Twelve Trees Junction which made its debut in October 2014 at the Great Electric Train Show. During 2015 it made one venture out in public when it appeared at the Great Central Railway Model Event in June representing the magazine. In a reflection of its busy nature a Bulleid 'Merchant Navy' accelerates through the junction to pass a Bulleid 'Q1' 0-6-0 while a 2-BIL and 2-HAL EMU combination arrives at the station behind. Twelve Trees Junction featured in HM97.
Mike Wild/Hornby Magazine.

DIGITAL SOUND

Making a 'Black Five' smoke!

Stanier's 'Black Five' was amongst the best of the mixed traffic designs and it has been immortalised by Hornby's popular model. **PAUL CHETTER** continues the 4-6-0 theme with the fitting of sound, smoke and stay-alive capacitor to Hornby's latest generation 'Black Five'.

Fitted with a Zimo MX645R sound decoder in the tender and a Seuthe smoke generator up front, this Hornby 'Black Five' offers a tremendous amount of operational value now.

HORNBY'S 'BLACK FIVE' has been around a while now but it remains a very good model that portrays these numerous and hard working locomotives well. Since its introduction Hornby has upgraded it to make it more suitable for sound installation with relocation of the decoder socket into the tender and provision in the chassis for the addition of a speaker.

The cutaway reveals that ample space to fit the required components for Digital Command Control (DCC) sound, smoke effects and stay-alive capacitor is available. The locomotive body and tender top each have only one fixing screw to be released to enable them to be removed from their chassis. In each case the superstructure must be raised at the front then slid backwards carefully to release securing lugs at the rear.

At the rear of the tender is a vacuum pipe. This is a push-fit into the buffer beam and should be removed before sliding the tender top backwards. If you don't, it will pop off, uncontrolled, anyway. The tender chassis features electrical pick ups on each wheel, a shaped metal casting to add weight and rigidity and an 8-pin DCC socket, with a blanking plate fitted for analogue operation without a decoder. To fit a standard motor decoder alone, all that is required is to remove the blanking plate, plug in the decoder, position it neatly and refit the tender top.

INSTALLING DCC SOUND IN A HORNBY 'BLACK FIVE'

1 Hornby's current format 'Black Five' with a tender mounted 8-pin decoder socket and provision for 28mm round speaker offers plenty of space for DCC sound, smoke and 'stay alive' installation.

2 This screw above the front bogie should be removed to release the front of the locomotive body. Raise the body until the chassis is clear at the front then slide it rearwards to disengage the rear locating lugs.

3 The red arrow points out the 4-pin connector whilst the yellow arrow indicates the single screw which must be released to allow the tender top to be raised at the front.

PLEASE TURN FOR MORE STEPS

Sound fitment

Hornby has provided a partial fitment for a downwards facing 28mm speaker in the chassis moulding. To add sound requires access to this area to fit the speaker. To do this the blanking plate needs to be removed along with the two screws holding the DCC connector. This reveals a chrome plated screw which, with the forward screw, must be removed to release the metal casting.

To obtain the best performance, the sound from the front of a speaker should be isolated from the equal but opposite sounds from the rear. The Hornby solution fixes the position of the speaker and allows the 'front' sound to escape downwards, but it does not isolate it from the rear sound. Consequently the out-of-phase sounds mix, largely cancelling each other resulting in low volume, poor quality output.

Fortunately, this is not difficult to fix provided you pay attention to detail. The gaps below the speaker in the central chassis channel, in the partially moulded ring and in the floor rearwards of the centre wheels must all be completely sealed. There are several ways to achieve this, but the simplest is to use a pliable material capable of bridging large gaps and holding itself in place. Black mastic is ideal for this, and many other fixing duties where a firm hold is needed but the permanence of glue is undesirable.

I secured the speaker with a continuous ring of mastic before soldering the purple wires from the Zimo MX645R sound decoder to the speaker connections as access later would be impeded. There should not be any contact between these connections and the cast metal, but if this did occur it would have catastrophic implications for the decoder's amplifier, so I used a short length of insulating tape to cover them.

I soldered additional wires to the DCC socket to provide power for the smoke generator. These were passed through a small hole I drilled in the tender floor near to the existing 4-pin connector. This position keeps the wires away from the tender wheels. The 4-pin connector services a plug-in wiring bridge between tender and locomotive to provide pick-up connections and power to the locomotive mounted motor.

I wound the additional wires around the existing wire bridge to provide support and camouflage before they entered the locomotive below the footplate. I used very flexible 'decoder' wire because many thin wire types have an insulation which is too stiff for this purpose and can cause poor riding characteristics and ultimately even provoke derailments. I threaded the decoder through the metal casting and secured all components in place, coiling the decoder harness before fitting the plug into the socket.

The MX645R decoder has onboard circuitry to manage external capacitors for stay–alive capability, improving reliability. This special circuit has a regulated voltage output regardless of that from the track, so lower voltage capacitors can be used safely. One or more capacitors wired in parallel could be added to the coal bunker, with a modified 'full' coal load used to hide them. I decided to use the Zimo SC68 supercapacitor, which will fit below the standard 'part used' coal load supplied with the model due to its size and format.

A couple of 0.8mm holes were drilled in the floor of the coal space through which I passed the blue and the grey capacitor wires from the decoder before soldering them to the SC68 connection tabs and covering with the coal load. The tender top and vacuum pipe were refitted in a reverse of the separation procedure completing the comprehensive installation work in this area.

Smoke installation

Zimo decoders have excellent onboard control of smoke generator output. The density of smoke can be varied automatically depending upon throttle position. At idle or on deceleration only light smoke is produced, when accelerating the maximum is emitted but when cruising a medium density plume coincides with modest regulator settings. The effects are more convincing than the simple on or off states common with other brands in my view.

The wires for the smoke unit previously installed in the tender were routed up and along the length of the boiler, held with mastic, where they would be soldered to the smoke generator's connectors and insulated with heatshrink tubing. To connect the smoke generator solder brown wire from the decoder to the brown wire on the smoke generator and the blue wire from the decoder to the yellow wire on the generator. In this installation we made these connections on the relevant pins on the decoder socket in the tender.

There is just enough height in the free space below the chimney to fit a Seuthe No. 22 smoke generator, but a small amount of work is required to be able to fit one to the model.

The chimney's internal opening is tapered as it passes down into the smokebox preventing the narrow portion of the generator from fitting. The hole should be opened out to approximately 5mm throughout its entire length and then the smoke unit will fit comfortably. You can use a drill bit for this, but I used a rounded warding file from below to obtain a snug fit holding the unit in place.

There is no access directly below the chimney, so in order to prepare the chimney opening and to be able to insert the smoke generator from below, I drilled a 13mm hole in the plastic below the chimney. Note that I removed the smokebox door so that I could illustrate the internal fitment clearly. There is no requirement to do this as a normal part of the installation.

The wires as they emerge from the smoke unit are easily damaged, so bend them into the correct position once only. I normally reinforce this with an epoxy adhesive, not shown in this feature. Reassembly is a reverse of the action on disassembly. Add some smoke fluid and away you go.

The 'Black Five' sound project is available from Digitrains and is already configured to operate variable smoke effects with a Seuthe No. 22 smoke unit if fitted. Installing these features really makes a difference to the model and takes its operational value into a new league. ■

INSTALLING DCC SOUND IN A HORNBY 'BLACK FIVE'

4 With the tension lock coupling removed, the screw indicated by the red arrow is visible. This does not need to be removed during this procedure. The yellow arrow highlights the vacuum pipe assembly which is in the way of the body sliding backwards.

5 If you slide the body backwards you will either damage the vacuum pipe or dislodge it from its mounting or both. Remove the pipe beforehand for a controlled release with no damage.

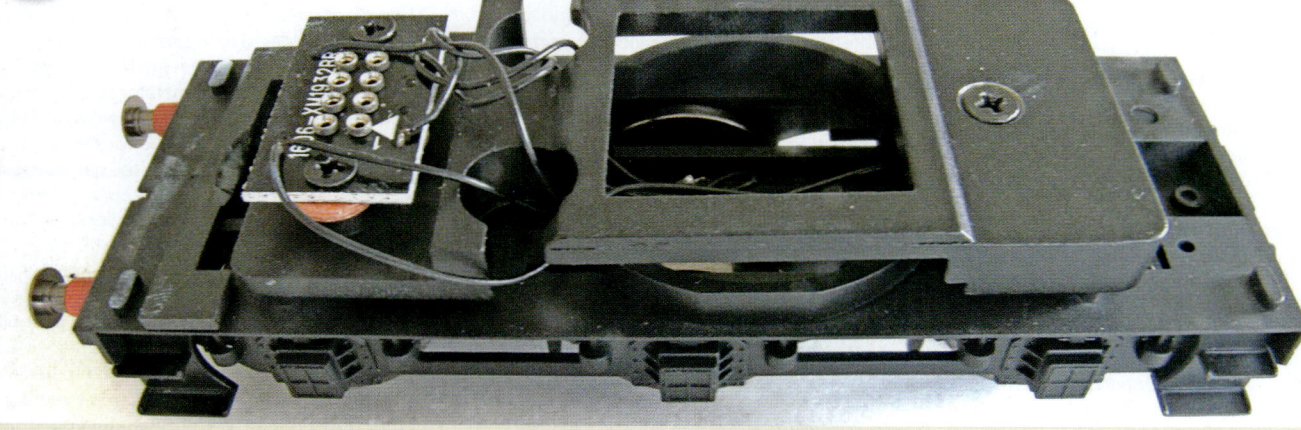

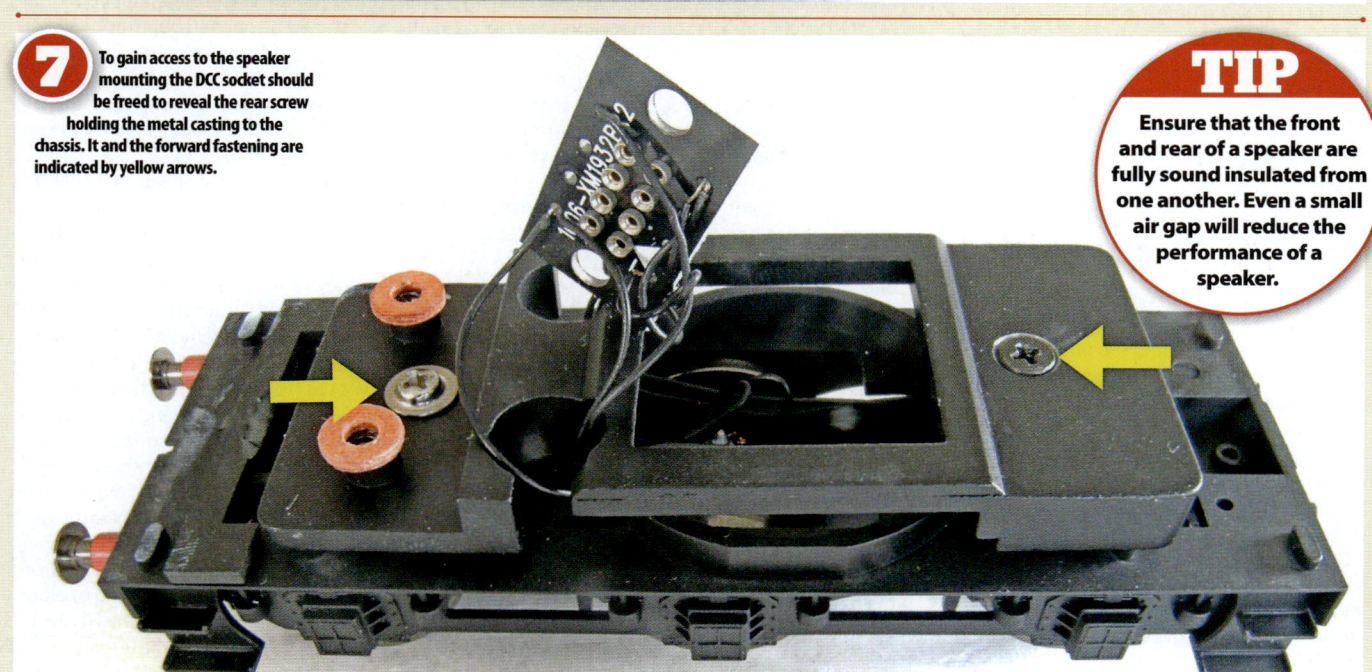

6 With the tender top removed the chassis, metal reinforcement and DCC socket can be seen. The blanking plate has been removed to show the socket securing screws. At this point, a simple DCC decoder installation only requires a decoder to be inserted and the tender reassembled.

7 To gain access to the speaker mounting the DCC socket should be freed to reveal the rear screw holding the metal casting to the chassis. It and the forward fastening are indicated by yellow arrows.

TIP
Ensure that the front and rear of a speaker are fully sound insulated from one another. Even a small air gap will reduce the performance of a speaker.

DIGITAL SOUND

WHAT WE USED

PRODUCT	SUPPLIER	PRICE
Zimo MX645R Sound Decoder	www.digitrains.co.uk	£83.00
28mm round speaker	www.digitrains.co.uk	£5.50
Zimo SC68 supercapacitor	www.digitrains.co.uk	£22.00
Seuthe No. 22 smoke generator	www.digitrains.co.uk	£23.08

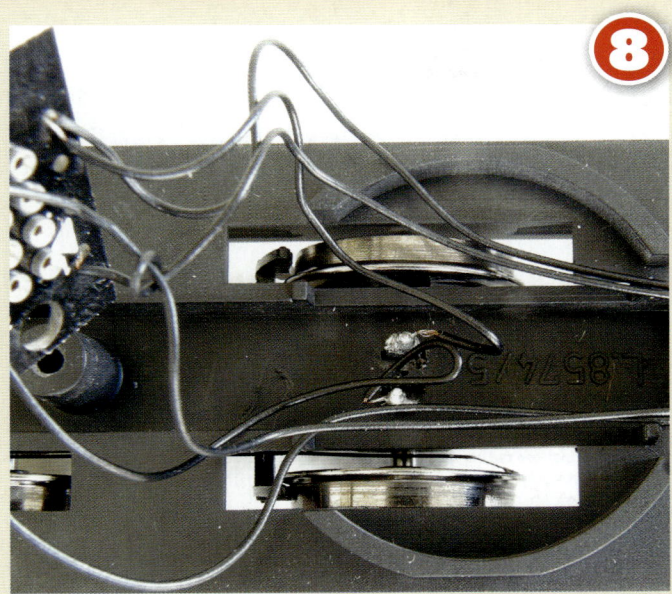

8 Below the casting this bundle of wires can be found loosely stuffed into the chassis channel where they might interfere with the face of the speaker. Secure them with sticky mastic or similar.

9 Here and in the previous picture can be seen the performance reducing gaps below and around the speaker, here loose fitted for a dry run.

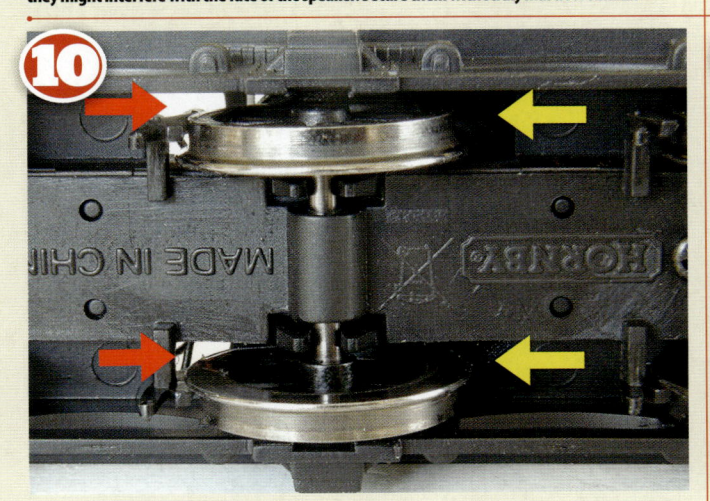

10 The same problem can be observed from below. The yellow arrows show the area of the speaker exposed to free access to the outside and the red arrows show the large gaps which will allow sound from the rear of the speaker to interfere with those from the front, reducing volume and quality in the sound reproduction.

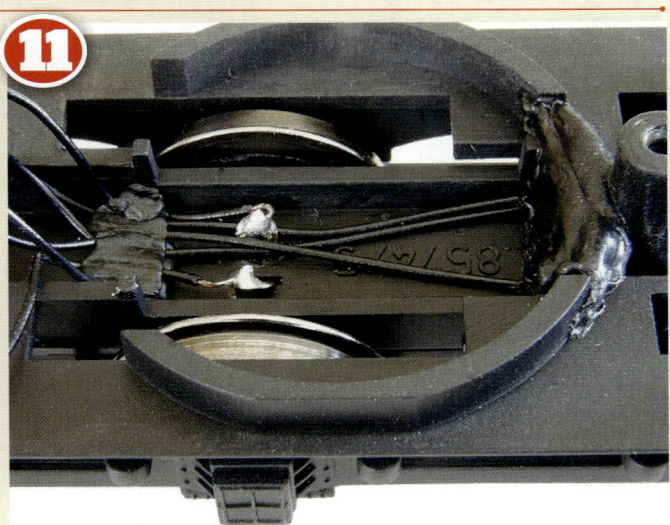

11 Mastic has been used to hold the wires in place and to build up gap filling layers in the central channel and speaker ring.

12 With the speaker in place, a ring of mastic seals it in and also covers the remaining gaps in the floor. Take care not to overfill these gaps: mastic should not touch the face of the speaker or make any contact with the wheels. Before refitting the metal casting, I soldered the decoder's speaker wires to the speaker ensuring that they were fully insulated from contact with the casting.

13 A pair of wires must run from the socket to the locomotive to power the smoke generator. A small hole was drilled inside the chassis channel close to the 4-pin plug which connects the locomotive and tender together for them to pass from inside the tender when reassembled. This position helps to keep the wires away from the wheels.

PLEASE TURN FOR MORE STEPS

INSTALLING DCC SOUND IN A HORNBY 'BLACK FIVE'

14 I threaded the decoder through the metal casting and put a coil in the decoder harness to facilitate reassembly later. The speaker terminals were protected from shorting by applying some insulating tape.

15 The plastic coal load can be easily removed revealing the large space available. A number of normal electrolytic capacitors would fit here and a new coal load could be fabricated to cover them.

16 I decided to use a Zimo SC68 supercapacitor instead. This packs 6800uF capacitance into a conveniently small, flat package.

17 Two 0.8mm holes drilled into the bunker floor allow the stay-alive wires from the MX645R decoder to pass through to meet the capacitor.

18 The blue positive wire was soldered to the single positive connector on the SC68 and the grey, negative, wire to one of a pair of connectors at the other end.

19 The capacitor is easily covered by the standard coal load moulding which, when the tender is reassembled, completes the work on the tender.

DIGITAL SOUND

20 The model is quite robust in most respects but these sand pipes are plastic and very fine. When the body has been removed they are vulnerable to damage so take great care not to break them.

21 From below and looking forwards the entrance of the smokebox and the lower portion of the chimney can be seen. Note the flat surface near the front fixing tower below the chimney.

22 I drilled a 13mm hole in this flat area through which I could open out the lower portion of the chimney with a small rounded file and then insert the smoke unit from below, taking care not to over stress the wires by bending them only once.

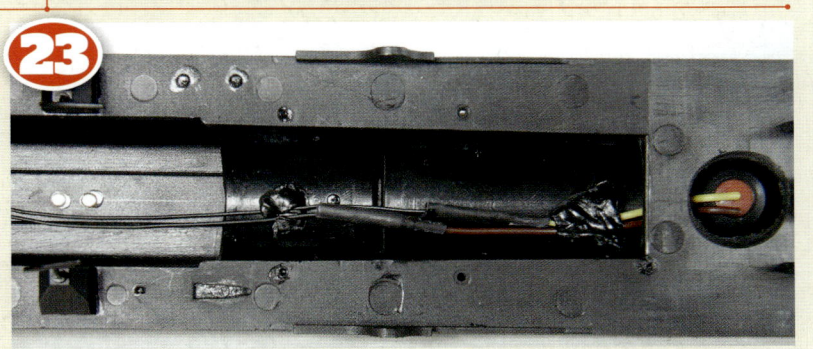

23 The fitted Seuthe No. 22 smoke generator can be seen in position from below and the power wires held in place with mastic. The brown wire connects to the brown wire on the decoder and the yellow wire to the blue wire on the decoder.

24 Don't do this at home! I removed the smokebox door so that you can clearly see the way it is fitted, but there is no need to do this to complete the installation.

25 Make sure the unit is centralised in the chimney and that it does not protrude above the rim of the chimney. Reassemble the locomotive body and chassis to complete the installation.

SCENERY

West Riding Power
Scenery

Every layout needs scenery to breathe realism and life into it. **MIKE WILD** continues the story of this year's project layout and explains how the bare boards were transformed.

Captured through the trees a Class 58 moves slowly through the discharge shed dropping the contents of its rake of HAA hoppers.

SCENERY

GROUND TEXTURE, contours, buildings and colours are all elements which go together to take our models from being merely track on a baseboard into a miniature world. Development of scenery is a very rewarding part of railway modelling and hosts a number of challenges as it bridges art, craft and DIY skills.

No scenic layout will ever be complete overnight – the drying times alone mean that is a physical impossibility – but while we have generated the scenic effects on West Riding Power over a couple of weeks, with time and patience detailed scenery is well within the reach of every modeller. In this feature we'll be showing tips and techniques which we use to assist in speeding up the process of scenic modelling and creating realistic finishes.

New methods

One of the first areas of the layout to be tackled when it comes to scenery is ballasting the track. All of our previous layouts have used the time honoured method of diluted PVA glue applied with a syringe to fix the ballast in place, but not West Riding Power. With the arrival of a new product via Gaugemaster of Deluxe Materials Ballast Magic we had the perfect opportunity to try something new.

This product is quite clever. It is powdered glue which can be mixed with any type of readily available ballast product and it takes a lot of the mess – and stress – out of model railway ballasting as it puts you firmly in control. The starter kit contains everything you need – a bottle of Ballast Magic powdered glue, a spray mister bottle, a measuring cup and a spatula for mixing the powder into ballast. All you have to add is your choice of ballast and fill the spray bottle with water.

The process of using this product is simple. We used a slightly stronger ratio of powder to ballast than recommended, opting for one part powder glue to four parts ballast using the supplied measuring cup to weigh it out. Having collected the right amounts of glue and ballast in a spare plastic tub and mixed it thoroughly the contents were carefully spread onto the layout dry over the track using just enough to cover the track and the cess between the running lines. This was then carefully brushed into place with a ½in paintbrush, just as we would do in traditional ballasting.

With a couple of drops of model oil on the point blades and mechanism to prevent them from sticking, the final step is to load the spray bottle with water and mist it over the powder laden ballast. After a few hours the ballast is dried solid in place with much less mess and fuss than traditional methods.

Using this method it took less than two hours to ballast the whole scenic section of West Riding Power – a significant time saving over traditional methods.

Landforms

With the theme of reducing the mess of model making firmly in mind we chose another new method for a *Hornby Magazine* layout when it came to creating the contours and landforms. Not to be wasteful either we used the packaging from the Bachmann Scenecraft buildings throughout production of the scenic contours!

The bulk of the landform is created by cutting strips of cardboard 10-15mm wide and weaving them together to create a web. This was stapled along the outer edges to stop pieces from separating during assembly and then fixed to the layout with PVA glue using track pins to temporarily hold the web in place while the glue dried.

This method made creating the landforms one of the cleanest jobs on the layout – a point that was further proven when we used a section of expanded polystyrene to make the contours on the left-hand corner. The resulting mess from trimming the polystyrene to shape made us appreciate the simplicity of the cardboard webbing!

Having completed all the ground contours all of the webbing was overlaid with masking tape to create a sealed surface onto which we could lay Gaugemaster plaster cloth which would in turn create a hard shell landscape suitable for adding colour and ground cover textures onto. The plaster cloth was laid carefully to avoid contact with the previously completed ballast and bridge structures until all the layout was covered. The banks of the riverbed were formed by rolling strips of plaster cloth into strips lengthways and pressing them into place along the edges of the river. Finally the whole landform was painted brown using poster paints.

Scenic detailing

While it is tempting to rush straight into the addition of ground cover textures like grass and bushes, the development of a scenic layout needs to be treated in layers, ensuring that each new layer overlaps the previous one for seamless joins.

First we created the roadways into the power station and down the gradient alongside the church. The base was created by cutting 1mm thick plasticard to shape and covering it with 1200grade wet and dry paper which gives a convincing look of tarmac. The road alongside the church was created from the same surface material, but laid directly onto the plaster cloth.

With these features done the next area of attention were the bridge supports. These had been left in plain plastic on purpose to avoid the final textures getting coloured with plaster or paint – although some plaster cloth had to be added carefully around the bridge supports after their completion.

The basic plastic boxes built from a sheet of 1mm thick plasticard were covered with Redutex brick texture sheets, available from DCC Supplies. These sheets, while not being budget items, are excellent products which feature textured brick finishes and a self adhesive backing which means they are very simple and quick to use. Each bridge support was covered with these with the relevant size pieces being cut out with scissors then fixed in place using their self adhesive backing. Simple.

With these features complete and in position ground cover could start. The first layer is Woodland Scenics blended green fine turf which is applied over a layer of neat PVA wood glue. Once dry the excess is removed which gives us a basic ground covering across the layout. To ensure the layers of grass and ballast blended together as we wanted the next application was weathering of the track using Geoscenics Track Grime colour applied from an airbrush. This pre-mixed colour is a simple means of applying single colour track weathering which can be done either before or after ballasting. Further colours could be added to the centre of the track if desired.

Taking the ground cover to the next level »

MiniNatur static grasses of 4.5mm and 6.5mm lengths in Autumn and Winter colours were applied next by spreading diluted PVA glue over the previously dried fine turf covering. This application was repeated in places adjusting the levels of Autumn and Winter coloured static grasses on a regular basis to keep variation in the tone of the grass.

Finishing touches

Driving the scenic side through to completion and giving it further depth are trees and bushes. The trees for the layout have been chosen to give it height and come from the Noch range supplied by Gaugemaster in the UK. Trees of choice are beech, oak, weeping willow and chestnut, offering a range of heights from 110mm to 195mm. These trees are all delivered fully finished and feature detailed leaf effects.

In total there are more than 15 large trees on West Riding Power which are further bedded in, particularly around the backscenes, with the ever useful Woodland Scenics fine leaf foliage in light green and olive green. This material is a superb way of representing small bushes and trees and has been used extensively on the layout to create features such as the dense hedgerow alongside the road next to the church as well as small bushes around the base of the main truss bridge at the centre of the layout.

Adding further to the texture a large coal heap has been developed around the sidings in the power station area. This has been created by mixing Woodland Scenics mine run coal with Deluxe Materials Ballast Magic and building up the heap in layers to achieve the final effect. The power station has also benefitted from detailed grass effects using static grass to bed in the buildings and road blending everything together.

One of the final elements to be added to the layout is fencing, all of which is Peco's flexible field fencing. Delivered on sprues it has to be assembled in lengths and additional support pieces fitted. It is designed to press together and while a little fiddly to do is quite effective once finished and easily adjusted to fit scenic contours.

The river

A regular feature of *Hornby Magazine's* recent exhibition layouts has been water and West Riding Power is no exception. Power stations are often sited near rivers and we wanted to use a watercourse to break up what would otherwise be a large expanse of greenery.

The riverbed was painted with Tamiya dark soil textured paint and edged with static grasses, fine and coarse turfs to create the river banks. Before applying the water materials the riverbed was fully prepared and each end was sealed so that the water wouldn't seep off on application. A word of caution here – always protect the floor when using products such as the Woodland Scenics realistic water as they have a habit of finding even the smallest gap to get through!

The final product to be applied before realistic water was a selection of grades of talus rocks from Woodland Scenics and coarse grade ballasts to represent stones and rocks along the river banks. This done, the first layer of realistic water was poured on to the recommended depth of $1/8$ in and left to cure.

The realistic water contracts on application, so it will always be thinner on drying than on application. To complete the water on West Riding Power we made a further four

WHAT WE USED		
PRODUCT	MANUFACTURER/SUPPLIER	CAT NO.
Chestnut tree, 195mm	Noch/Gaugemaster	21800
Willow tree, 110mm	Noch/Gaugemaster	21770
Beech tree, 130mm	Noch/Gaugemaster	21690
Oak tree, 160mm	Noch/Gaugemaster	21760
Plaster cloth	Gaugemaster	GM100
Ballast Magic	Deluxe Materials/Gaugemaster	AD76/AD74
Blended green fine turf	Woodland Scenics	T1349
Light green coarse turf	Woodland Scenics	WT1363
Burnt grass coarse turf	Woodland Scenics	WT1362
Light green fine leaf foliage	Woodland Scenics	WF1132
Olive green fine leaf foliage	Woodland Scenics	WF1133
Realistic water	Woodland Scenics	WC1211
Medium grey talus	Woodland Scenics	WC1279
Blended grey coarse ballast	Woodland Scenics	WB1395
Blended grey fine ballast	Woodland Scenics	WD1393
Mine run coal	Woodland Scenics	WB92
Masking tape	B&Q	
1mm thick plasticard	Evergreen	9040
1200grade wet and dry paper	Titan	98101
Flexible field fencing	Peco	NB-45
Dry stone walling	Javis	PW1N
Self adhesive brick texture sheets	Redutex	148LV122

Static grasses help to detail the foreground while the height of the Noch trees at the rear of the layout gives a sense of scale to the model.

applications of realistic water to build up the depth to the level we wanted. Each layer needs at least 24 hours to cure so this was a time consuming part of the project we left until the end when minimal scenic work remained to be done reducing the chance of stray grass fibres and turfs landing in semi-cured water.

Realism

No layout is ever really complete and there is plenty which can be done to West Riding Power in the future to further enhance the detail and quality of the scenery. Further fencing, maybe a flock of sheep in the corner of a field and other features could all be built in to improve it further.

The result now is a pleasing layout which looks how we wanted it to with tall trees in the background surrounding open green fields with the power station buildings rising up from the ground behind. Now all we need to do is complete the detailing and weathering of the rolling stock to match the quality of the layout.

Turn to pages 112-119 to read more about the operation and rolling stock. ■

BUILDING WEST RIDING POWER'S SCENERY

SKILL LEVEL: Beginner / Intermediate / Advanced

1 The first step is ballasting. For this project we are using Deluxe Materials new Ballast Magic powder adhesive supplied by Gaugemaster and Woodland Scenics fine grade blended grey ballast.

2 Before any ballasting can be done the gaps in the sleeper formation where lengths of track join need to be filled. Peco produces sleepers especially for this task in 'N' gauge which are simply cut from their sprue with a craft knife and glued in place with contact adhesive. More care needs to be taken around points where the angles mean that some of the sleeper ends will need to be removed so they fit correctly.

3 Measure out one part of Ballast Magic adhesive powder using the measuring cup provided in the starter kit and tip it into a larger mixing bowl…

4 …next, four parts of ballast are measured out using the same measuring cup and then tipped into the mixing bowl. The two products can now be stirred together dry so that it is ready to apply to the layout.

5 Ballast is spread onto the layout over the track formation and carefully brushed into place so it forms a neat 'shoulder' around the track.

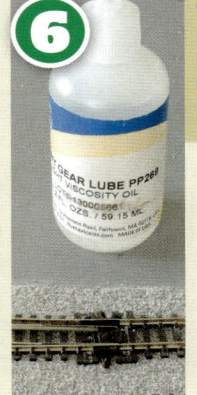

6 To ensure that the points don't get glued in place a couple of drops of model oil are placed on the mechanism and around the ends of the tie bars as a precaution.

7 Using the spray bottle from the Ballast Magic starter kit the previously laid dry ballast and powder mixture is wetted and then left to dry. Once dry it will be set in place offering neat, simple and clean ballasting.

SCENERY

BUILDING WEST RIDING POWER'S SCENERY

SKILL LEVEL: Intermediate (Beginner / Advanced)

8. With ballasting complete attention turns to the landforms. The majority of the contours on this layout have been formed using a web of cardboard strips. Staples were used to pin the edges together during assembly and they were fixed to the layout using PVA glue with track pins used to secure the webs during drying of the glue.

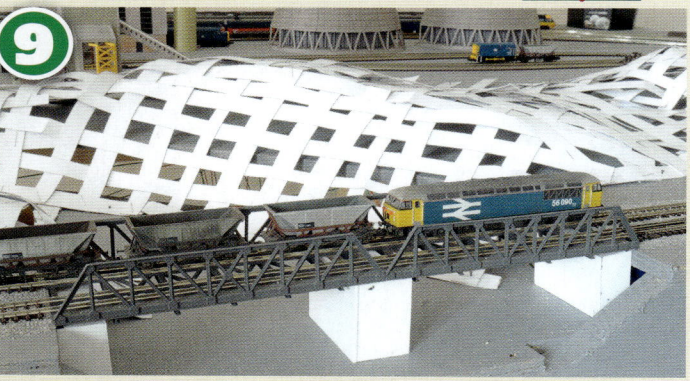

9. The landforms add great depth to the scenery and are a quick, clean and cheap means of creating basic scenic structures. The cardboard was obtained by using the packaging from the Scenecraft buildings for the layout.

10. To create a sealed surface onto which plaster bandage can be applied the entire landform was covered with masking tape. This also adds strength and bonds the strips of card together.

11. The entire landform was then covered with Gaugemaster plaster bandage. Multiple layers were built up over the model – two in most places and three where required – to provide a hard wearing base for scenic detailing.

12. Next the now dried landform was painted brown with poster paints. Areas of plaster remain to be completed around the bridge at this point as the supports were still being made.

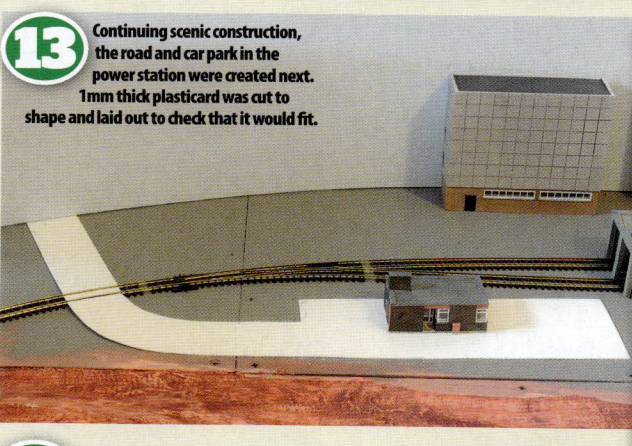

13. Continuing scenic construction, the road and car park in the power station were created next. 1mm thick plasticard was cut to shape and laid out to check that it would fit.

14. The road surface was then added using 1200grade wet and dry paper glued to the plastic sheets with contact adhesive.

15. The bridge supports, made from 1mm thick plasticard and glued together with Deluxe Materials Plastic Magic, were covered with Redutex self adhesive textured brick sheets. This material is a joy to work with and provides a superb pre-painted detailed finish.

16. The Redutex sheets stand close scrutiny and can be cut with scissors to suit shapes. The flexibility of the material also means a single piece can be used to wrap around a structure like this central support for the truss bridge.

17. With the pillars complete and glued in place with contact adhesive the plaster bandage surface around the bridge footings was completed and then painted in the same colour as the rest of the landform.

www.hornbymagazine.com 83

SCENERY

A Class 37 rounds the curve above the church with a rake of Presflos. The hedge row has been assembled from pieces of Woodland Scenics fine leaf foliage.

18 On other parts of the layout the first layer of ground cover was going down using PVA adhesive to fix it in place. The starting point is a layer of Woodland Scenics blended green fine turf which looks quite stark at this stage.

19 An important part of scenic development is taking a step back to see how elements will sit together. Here a selection of Noch trees supplied by Gaugemaster are positioned along the backscene to see how their height will work with 'N' gauge rolling stock.

20 Continuing the layered approach to the scenery the track was weathered next with Geoscenics track grime before the top layers of grasses were applied. The weathering was applied with an airbrush for speed.

21 Building up the scenery, Woodland Scenics light green fine leaf foliage was placed along the backscenes to create depth and height at this visual barrier. The pieces of foliage are fixed in place with PVA glue.

SCENERY

BUILDING WEST RIDING POWER'S SCENERY

SKILL LEVEL: Intermediate

22 Trees are temporarily placed in front of the hedging to gauge their appearance and where more pieces of fine leaf foliage are required to enhance the joint between the baseboard and backscene.

Taken immediately after completion of the static grass layers and before adding hedge rows and extra grass textures, the greenery on West Riding Power looks smart but stark. It is the details which lift this basic texture to the next level.

23 With a layer of diluted PVA wood glue MiniNatur autumn and winter coloured static grasses were applied next and the trees added using neat PVA glue to complete this area. Static grasses were used across the rest of the layout to increase the depth and texture of the grassed areas.

24 With the excess materials vacuumed away the static grasses give good texture to the scene but will benefit from further layers of scenic detailing at a later stage.

25 With fine leaf foliage creating a hedge row between the railway and road, static grass detailing to the green areas and trees from Noch the scenic area is developing nicely. It's all about adding layers on top of each other to build up a detailed finish.

26 The riverbed was painted with Tamiya dark earth textured paint and on top of this a mixture of grades of ballast and talus from Woodland Scenics were added loose to represent rocks around the river edge.

27 Having sealed the ends of the riverbed Woodland Scenics realistic water was poured onto the layout in thin layers to build up the water effect. Allowing 24hours for each coat to dry, four layers were added in total to create the final look.

SCENERY

28 The river banks were detailed with fine leaf foliage glued in place with PVA glue and Woodland Scenics coarse and fine turf fixed with extra strong hair spray – a quick and clean way of adding extra scenic layers.

29 The finishing touches were Peco flexible fencing along the railway and power station boundaries fitted into 1mm diameter holes drilled in the baseboard and scenic surface.

TIP
Developing ground cover is all about building up layers. Using this method each new layers softens the previous one blending it into the overall scene. For more on ground cover techniques see Nigel Burkins feature on pages 12-19 of this Yearbook.

30 There is always more which can be done and we will no doubt come back to this layout in the future, but for now it is looking the part and could easily be overdone.

TRAIN FORMATIONS

EXPRESS

The glamorous express passenger trains are always popular on model railways. **MARK CHIVERS** examines some typical train formations from the 1950s to the 1980s.

EXPRESS PASSENGER TRAINS revolutionised travel around the country by slashing journey times between major towns and cities, encouraging people to undertake trips to destinations they might not have considered previously. Ever-mindful of the marketing opportunities, the railway companies capitalised on these quicker journeys, advertising headline timings showing just how quick their services were.

Many expresses covered long distances with limited stops at principal stations, which allowed onward connections to be made. Timetables were compiled to ensure that branch line and secondary services would feed

PASSENGER

TRAIN FORMATIONS

into and out of the main line expresses, offering attractive journey times to potential customers.

Expresses have generally always received the newest and best rolling stock and in the 1950s British Railways turned to its new Mk 1 coaches to compete more effectively with road travel. However, many pre-nationalisation vehicles remained in service and some had long lives.

Not all long distance express trains were formed the same way, with some featuring extra First Class accommodation, kitchen facilities and cooked meals. Some offered a buffet for part of the journey and others featured no catering facilities at all. Some regions also maintained dedicated coaching stock for specific express duties, such as the Southern Region's extensive boat train traffic.

Railway companies developed ever more powerful locomotives designed specifically for long distance express trains including the Great Western Railway (GWR) 'Castle' and 'King' 4-6-0s, Southern Railway (SR) 'Lord Nelson' 4-6-0s, 'Merchant Navy' and 'Battle of Britain'/'West Country' 4-6-2s, London, Midland & Scottish Railway (LMS) 'Princess Coronation' 4-6-2s, 'Royal Scot' and 'Jubilee' 4-6-0s and ex-London and North Eastern Railway (LNER) 'A1', 'A2', 'A3' and 'A4' 4-6-2s. As the transition from steam gathered pace, new diesel and electric locomotives appeared at the head of BR's express passenger services.

Double-chimney Gresley 'A3' 60096 *Papyrus* passes through Hookhills cutting on the climb to the Forth Bridge with an up express in 1959.
W.J. Verden Anderson/Rail Archive Stephenson.

Ready-to-run

Manufacturers have ensured a steady stream of these glamorous locomotives ready-to-run in 'OO' gauge, together with suitable matching rolling stock where possible, including Bachmann's recent LMS Porthole stock, GWR Collett, SR Bulleid and LNER Thompson coaches and an extensive selection of BR Mk 1 and Mk 2 carriage types. Hornby's 'OO' gauge range of coaches includes GWR Hawksworth, SR Maunsell, LMS 57ft Stanier Period III and LNER Gresley 61ft 6in coaches, together with examples of its newly-tooled Mk 2e air-conditioned vehicles and BR Mk 1, Mk 2d, Mk 3 and Mk 4 coaches, offering a wide selection of modelling opportunities. Other manufacturers have also produced useful coach types such as Dapol's 'OO' gauge LMS Stanier 60ft Composite (CK) and Replica Railways' BR Mk 1 First Open (FO) and BR Mk 1 Restaurant Buffet (RBR).

One area that is currently poorly served is provision of appropriate catering vehicles. As BR replaced much of its inherited pre-nationalisation fleet it retained a large number of elderly catering cars to provide refreshments on these long distance trains. These were gradually replaced by BR Mk 1 types but it was a slow process and as a result, it is not currently possible to fully replicate some of the following train formations with accurate catering facilities using ready-to-run products.

For the ultimate in authenticity kits are available for some of these missing vehicle types. However, Bachmann's RFO, RU and RMB vehicles together with the Mainline/Replica BR Mk 1 RBR are reasonable substitutes. Hornby's catering vehicles include a LMS 12-wheel dining car and LNER Gresley buffet car, both of which can be utilised to provide appropriate accommodation.

The following train formations represent a small snapshot of long-distance express passenger trains from the 1950s to 1980s and whilst they have been researched using prototype information, some have been shortened for 'OO' gauge as the formations often exceeded ten vehicles. Inevitably, an element of compromise has been necessary but where possible we have kept formations to a maximum of 12 carriages, although this could be further reduced by removing one or more similar vehicle types, to suit your layout. ∎

WESTERN

GWR 'King' 4-6-0 BR lined green, late crests (Hornby), BR Mk 1 BSK, FK, FK, RB, SK, SK, SK, BSK – BR chocolate and cream.
DATE: 1958 **SERVICE:** Kingswear–London Paddington

GWR 'Castle' 4-6-0 BR lined green, early crests (Hornby), BR Mk 1 BG, BG, CK, SK*, SK, SK, BSK – BR maroon except * BR chocolate and cream.
DATE: 1959 **SERVICE:** Neyland–London Paddington

GWR 'Castle' 4-6-0 BR lined green, late crests (Bachmann), BR Mk 1 BSK*, SK, SK, CK, CK, Gresley RB*, BR Mk 1 SO, SK, SK, BSK, SK, SK – BR carmine and cream except * BR maroon. **DATE:** 1962 **SERVICE:** Kingswear–Bradford

Class 47 BR two-tone green (Bachmann/Heljan/ViTrains), **Class 52 'Western'** BR maroon (Dapol/Heljan), BR Mk 1 BSK, SO, SO, RB, FO, FK, FK, FK, BSK – BR blue and grey
DATE: 1968 **SERVICE:** London Paddington–Bristol Temple Meads

Class 52 'Western' BR blue (Dapol/Heljan), BR Mk 2a TSO, TSO, TSO, BSO, BSO, FK, BR Mk 1 RB, FO, BR Mk 2a TSO, BFK – BR blue and grey
DATE: 1974 **SERVICE:** London Paddington–Penzance

Class 50 BR 'large logo' blue (Hornby), BR Mk 1 BG, BR Mk 2d-f FO, TSO, TSO, TSO, TSO, BR Mk 1 RBR – BR blue and grey.
DATE: 1985 **SERVICE:** London Paddington–Penzance

SOUTHERN

SR 'Lord Nelson' 4-6-0 BR lined green, late crests (Bachmann), Bulleid BSK, SK, CK, SK, BSK, BSK, CK, BSK, BSK, CK, BSK – BR green
DATE: 1962 **SERVICE:** London Waterloo–Bournemouth

SR rebuilt 'Merchant Navy' 4-6-2 BR lined green, late crests (Hornby), Bulleid BSK, CK, BSK, Maunsell CK, SK, Bulleid BSK, SK, CK, SK, BSK – BR green
DATE: 1962 **SERVIC:** London Waterloo–Bournemouth

SR rebuilt 'West Country' 4-6-2 BR lined green, late crests (Hornby), BR Mk 1 BSK, CK, SO, SO, RB, SO, SK, CK, BSK – BR green
DATE: 1962 **SERVICE:** Bournemouth–York

BR '5MT' 4-6-0 BR lined black, late crests (Bachmann), SR Bogie Van B, SR Bogie Van B, BR Mk 1 BSK, FK, FK, FK, FO, SO, SO, BSK – BR green
DATE: 1964 **SERVICE:** Southampton Docks–London Waterloo boat train

Class 419 Motor Luggage Van, BR Mk 1 BG (TLV)*, two **Class 411 4-CEP Electric Multiple Units** (Bachmann) – BR green except * BR blue and grey
DATE: 1968 **SERVICE:** London Victoria–Dover Marine boat train

Class 33/1 BR blue (Heljan), BR Mk 1 TSO, TSO, BSK, FK, RMB, TSO, TSO, TSO – BR blue and grey
DATE: 1979 **SERVICE:** Weymouth Quay–London Waterloo

TRAIN FORMATIONS

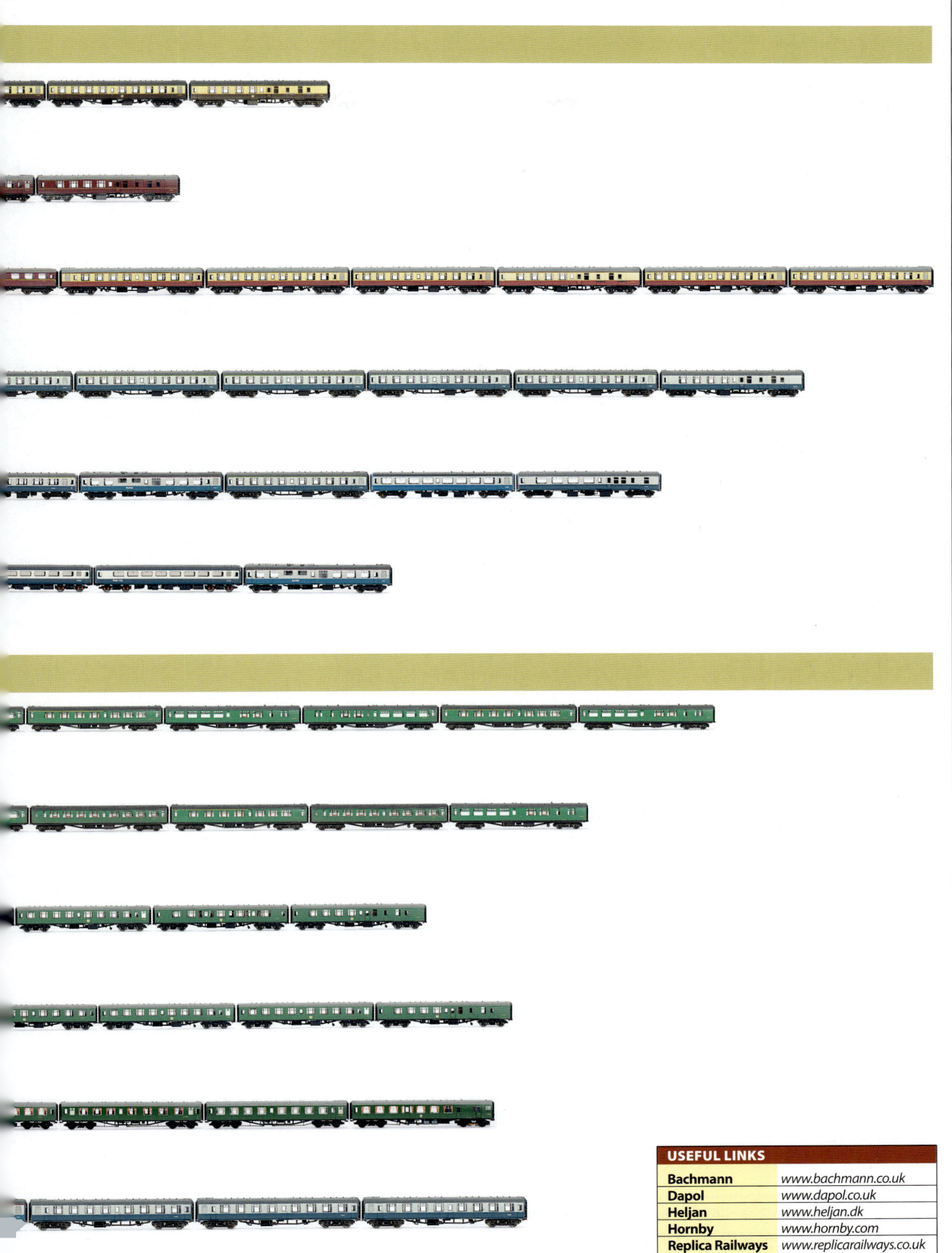

www.hornbymagazine.com

USEFUL LINKS	
Bachmann	www.bachmann.co.uk
Dapol	www.dapol.co.uk
Heljan	www.heljan.dk
Hornby	www.hornby.com
Replica Railways	www.replicarailways.co.uk

TRAIN FORMATIONS

Class 55 55017 *The Durham Light Infantry* runs beside the North Sea near Burnmouth with a nortbound express in 1976. The train is formed of air-conditioned Mk 2 vehicles. W.J. Verden Anderson/Rail Archive Stephenson.

MIDLAND

LMS 'Black Five' 4-6-0 BR black, late crests (Hornby), BR Mk 1 BSK, SK, SK, FO, RB, CK, SK, BSK, SK – BR maroon
DATE: 1959 **SERVICE:** Manchester Central–London St Pancras

LMS 'Princess Coronation' 4-6-2 BR lined green, early crests (Hornby), BR Mk 1 CK, SK, RU, CK, FK, BSK, BCK, SK, SK – BR maroon
DATE: 1961 **SERVICE:** Glasgow Central–London Euston

LMS 'Jubilee' 4-6-0 BR lined green, late crests (Bachmann), BR Mk 1 BSK, SK, CK, SK, BSK, RKB, FO, SK – BR maroon
DATE: 1961 **SERVICE:** Derby–London St Pancras

LMS rebuilt 'Patriot' 4-6-0 BR lined green, late crests (Bachmann/Hornby), Stanier BSK, CK, BR Mk 1 SK, SK, SK, SK, SK, SK, BSK, Stanier 50ft BG – BR maroon
DATE: 1963 **SERVICE:** London Euston–Liverpool Lime Street

Class 45 BR blue (Bachmann), BR Mk 2d-f BSO, TSO, TSO, TSO, BR Mk 1 RBR, Mk 2 d-f FO, FO – BR blue and grey
DATE: 1976 **SERVICE:** Sheffield–London St Pancras

Class 43 HST power car (Hornby), BR Mk 3 TF, TF, TRSB, TS, TS, TS, TGS, Class 43 HST power car (Hornby) – BR blue and grey
DATE: 1983 **SERVICE:** London St Pancras-Nottingham

TRAIN FORMATIONS

www.hornbymagazine.com

With a uniform rake of BR lined maroon Mk 1 carriages behind, Stanier 'Princess Coronation' 4-6-2 46242 *City of Glasgow* climbs Camden bank with a Down express on September 16 1960. David Hepburne-Scott/Rail Archive Stephenson.

'Castle' 4-6-0 7027 *Thonbury Castle* leaves Box Tunnel with a Paddington-Bristol express on May 27 1956 formed of Hawksworth and BR Mk 1 carriages. David Hepburne-Scott/Rail Archive Stephenson.

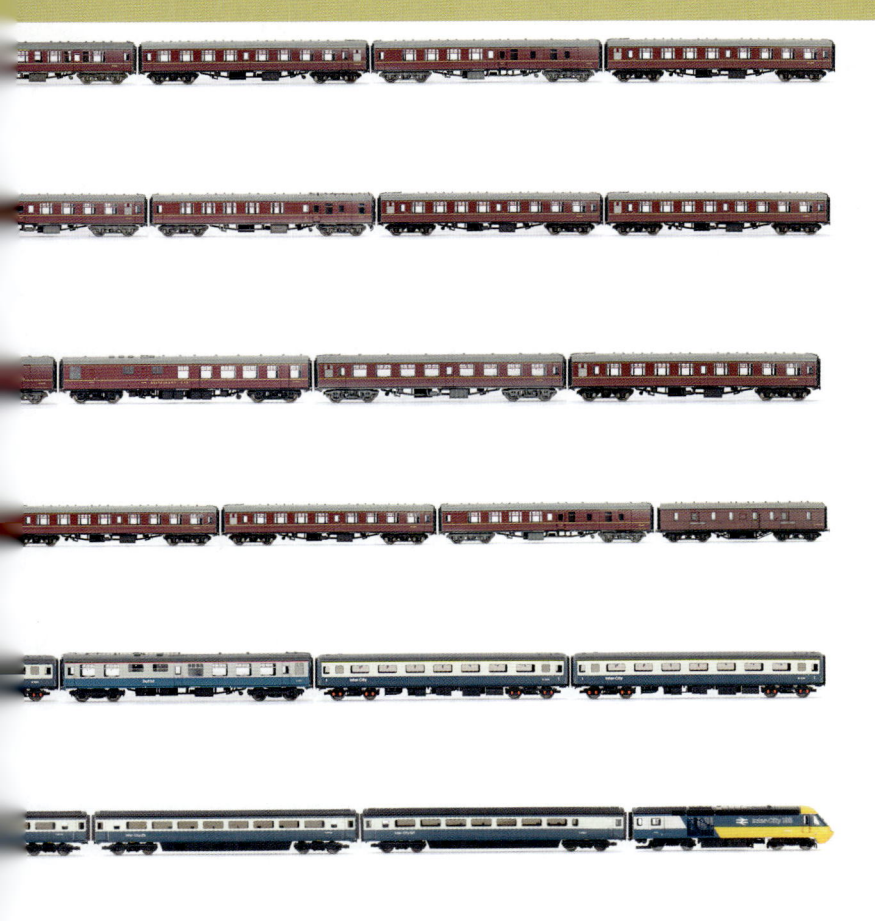

COACHING STOCK DESIGNATIONS	
BCK	Corridor Brake Composite
BFK	Corridor Brake First
BSK	Corridor Brake Second
BTK	Corridor Brake Third
BSO	Open Brake Second
CK	Corridor Composite
FK	Corridor First
FO	Open First
POS	Post Office Sorting Van
RB	Restaurant Buffet
RBR	Restaurant Buffet (refurbished)
RFO	Restaurant First (no kitchen)
RK	Kitchen Car
RKB	Kitchen Buffet
RMB	Miniature Buffet
RSP	Pantry Second
RU	Restaurant Unclassed
RUO	Restaurant Unclassed (kitchen)
RSO	Restaurant Second (no kitchen)
SK	Corridor Second
SO	Open Second
TF	Trailer First
TK	Corridor Third
TLV	Trailer Luggage Van
TO	Open Third
TRSB	Trailer Restaurant Standard Buffet
TS	Trailer Standard
TSO	Tourist Open Second

EASTERN

LNER 'A1' 4-6-2 BR lined green, early crests (Bachmann), Gresley 61ft 6in BG, FK, SK, SK, SK, RB, SK, SK, BCK - BR maroon
DATE: 1956 **SERVICE:** Edinburgh Waverley–London King's Cross

LNER 'A3' 4-6-2 BR lined green, late crests (Hornby), Gresley 61ft 6in BCK*, BR Mk 1 SK, SK, SK, TSO, FK, FK, CK, BSK – BR carmine and cream except * BR maroon
DATE: 1955 **SERVICE:** London King's Cross–Edinburgh Waverley

LNER 'A4' 4-6-2 BR lined green, late crests (Bachmann/Hornby), BR Mk 1 TSO, SK, BSK, CK, CK, FO, RU, CK, TSO, Gresley 61ft 6in SK, BR Mk 1 BSK – BR maroon
DATE: 1962 **SERVICE:** Newcastle–London King's Cross

Class 37/0 BR blue (Bachmann), BR Mk 2a FK, BSO, TSO, TSO, FK, BR Mk 1 RBR, BR Mk 2a FK, TSO, TSO, BSO – BR blue and grey
DATE: 1978 **SERVICE:** Norwich-London Liverpool Street

Class 55 'Deltic' BR blue (Bachmann), BR Mk 2d-f SO, SO, SO, SO, SO, SO, BR Mk 1 RBR, BR Mk 2d-f FO, FO, FO, BR Mk 1 BG – BR blue and grey
DATE: 1978 **SERVICE:** Aberdeen–London King's Cross

Class 47 BR blue (Bachmann/Heljan/ViTrains), BR Mk 1 BG, BG, BR Mk 2a FK, BR Mk 2d-f FO, BR Mk 1 RMB, BR Mk 2d-f TSO, TSO, TSO, TSO, BSO
DATE: 1984 **SERVICE:** Cambridge–London Liverpool Street

SCOTTISH

LMS 'Black Five' 4-6-0 BR black, late crests, LMS 'Black Five' BR black, late crests (Hornby), BR Mk 1 SK, BSK, CK, BSK, Thompson SK*, BR Mk 1 CK*, Gresley 61ft 6in SK, BR Mk 1 BSK, SK, SK* - BR maroon except * BR carmine and cream
DATE: 1960 **SERVICE:** Perth–Inverness

BR '8P' 4-6-2 *Duke of Gloucester* BR lined green, late crests (Hornby), Stanier BSK, FK, SK, SK, BSK – BR maroon
DATE: 1961 **SERVICE:** Aberdeen–Glasgow Buchanan Street

Class 26 BR green (Heljan), BR Mk 1 BSK, Stanier SK, BR Mk 1 CK, SK, SK, SK, Stanier 50ft BG – BR maroon
DATE: 1964 **SERVICE:** Dundee – Glasgow Buchanan Street

LNER 'A4' 4-6-2 BR lined green, late crests (Bachmann/Hornby), BR Mk 1 BSK, SK, CK, RMB, SK, SK, BG – BR maroon
DATE: 1965 **SERVICE:** Aberdeen–Glasgow Buchanan Street

Class 45 BR blue (Bachmann/Heljan/ViTrains), BR Mk 1 BCK, BR Mk 2a FK, BR Mk 1 RMB, BR Mk 2a TSO, TSO, BSO, TSO – BR blue and grey
DATE: 1981 **SERVICE:** Aberdeen-Edinburgh Waverley

Class 47 BR InterCity 'executive' (Bachmann), BR Mk 1 BG*, RBR, BR Mk 3 TSO, TSO, TSO, TSO, TSO, FO, BR Mk 1 BG – BR InterCity 'executive' except * BR blue and grey
DATE: 1986 **SERVICE:** Inverness-London Euston

TRAIN FORMATIONS

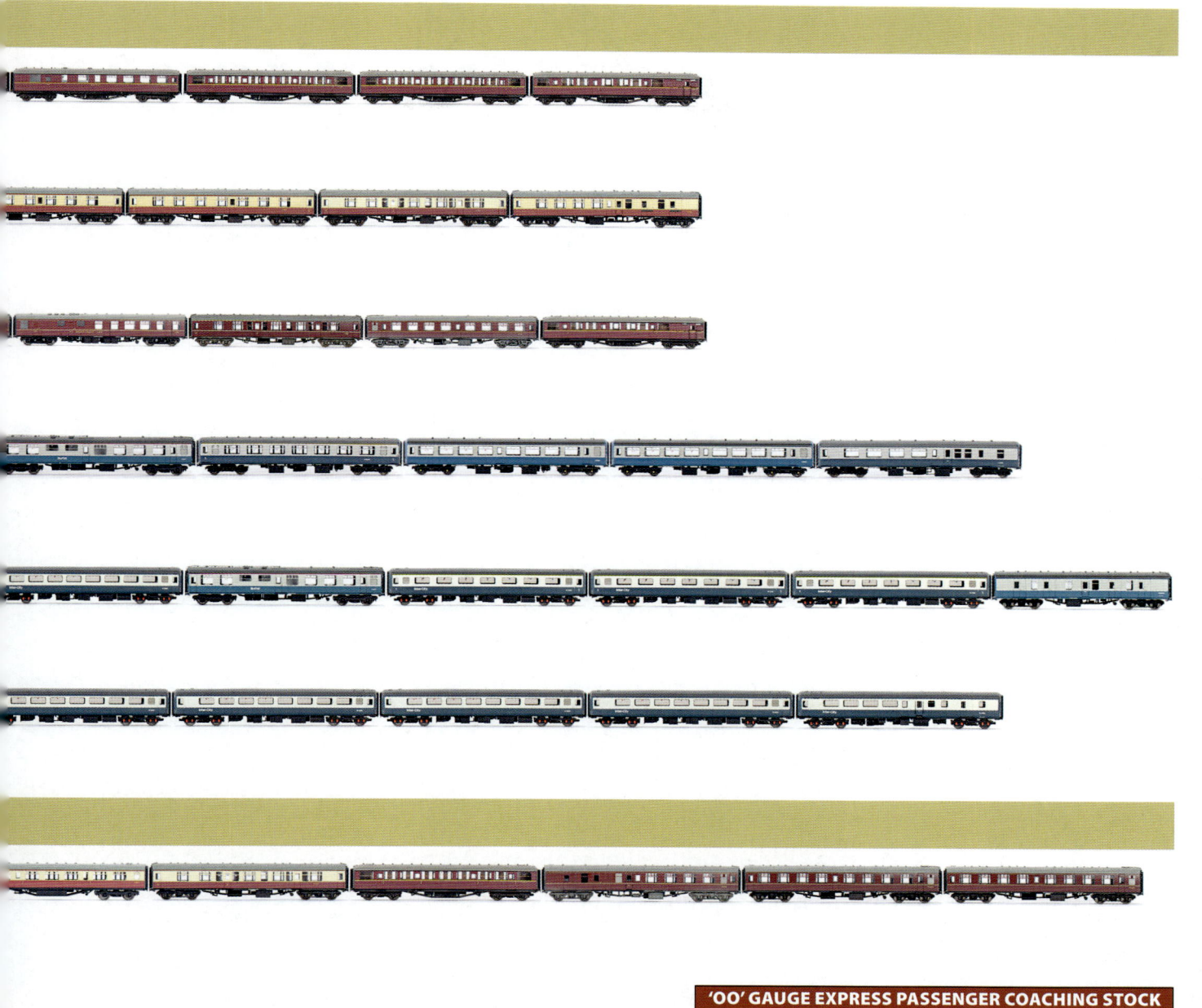

www.hornbymagazine.com

'OO' GAUGE EXPRESS PASSENGER COACHING STOCK	
TYPE	**MANUFACTURER**
BR Mk 1 carriages	Bachmann/Hornby/Replica
BR Mk 2/2a carriages	Bachmann
BR Mk 2d/2e carriages	Hornby
BR Mk 3 carriages	Hornby
BR Mk 4 carriages	Hornby
GWR 60ft Collett carriages	Bachmann
GWR Centenary carriages	Hornby
GWR Hawksworth carriages	Hornby
LMS Period Two 12-wheel dining car	Hornby
LMS Porthole carriages	Bachmann
LMS Stanier Period Three carriages	Dapol
LMS Stanier Period Three carriages	Hornby
LNER Gresley 61ft 6in carriages	Hornby
LNER Thompson carriages	Bachmann
SR Bulleid carriages	Bachmann
SR Maunsell carriages	Hornby
SR Bogie Van B, Van C	Hornby
SR PLV, PMV, CCT	Bachmann

Review of the Year 2014-2015

The last 12 months have seen a hectic pace of development in the modelling world. **MARK CHIVERS** tracks the changes and reveals the highlights since *Hornby Magazine* Yearbook No. 7.

HM88, October 2014  | HM89, November 2014  | HM90, December 2014   | HM91, January 2015  | HM92, Febuary 2015  | HM93, March 2015  | HM94, April 2015

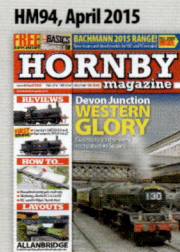

REVIEW OF THE YEAR

IT HAS BEEN ANOTHER YEAR of exciting developments with plenty of new model arrivals, a new manufacturer entering the market and even a number of duplicated model projects being announced, which has become something of a trend over the past 12 months.

Consideration of new projects and consolidation of others appears to have enabled the manufacturers to get back on track with their programmes of development, while improvements to the supply chain and increasing the portfolio of suppliers has enabled Hornby to deliver an impressive flow of new products throughout the year.

The lines continue to blur between retailer and manufacturer with plenty of new projects in the pipeline from Hattons of Liverpool and Kernow Model Rail Centre, while 2014 also saw the welcome arrival of Oxford Rail adding its name to the list of British outline model railway manufacturers and unveiling its first series of ready-to-run 'OO' gauge projects. The company is well versed in model manufacturing with its extensive range of Oxford Diecast scale model road vehicles.

Another very exciting development during the year was the arrival of Hornby's 'OO' gauge Twin Track Sound (TTS) fitted steam and diesel models. Offering the benefits of sound fitted locomotives at a much reduced price to previous factory fitted Digital Command Control (DCC) sound models, they have proved very popular with a number of the steam models selling very quickly. Providing an entry level product such as this was inspired and will certainly encourage more to sample the higher end DCC sound products as confidence continues to grow in this sector of the market.

Modelling of London's Underground (LU) network has also enjoyed a renaissance this year with the arrival of Heljan's 'OO' gauge Metropolitan Bo-Bo electric locomotive and a surprise 'OO' gauge release from the London Transport Museum of LU's most recent S Stock sub surface trains, as manufacturers and retailers explore other avenues to model.

It really has been a busy year, with a strong line-up of new models appearing each month as you will see in this look back at the year's significant releases. »

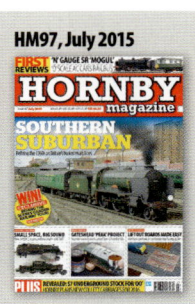

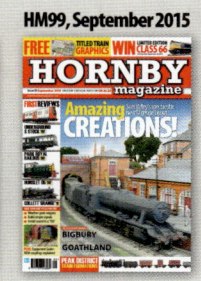

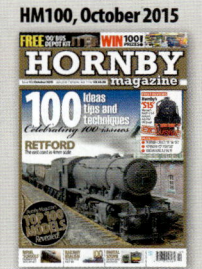

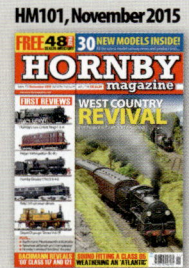

Locomotion Models' GNR Ivatt 'Atlantic' made its debut in April 2015. This stunning model was produced by Bachmann.

Bachmann's Billinton 'E4' 0-6-2T for 'OO'.

September 2014

Our review of the year starts with the arrival of Hornby's stunning main range version of its 'OO' gauge Gresley 'P2' 2-8-2 2001 *Cock O' the North* in LNER lined green featuring additional decoration over the previously released RailRoad model with lining around the cab, running plate, bufferbeam, wheels and axle boxes. Added to this were silver painted handrails, 'gold leaf' numbers with crisply printed red and black shadows together with a set of separate nameplates for placing over the printed versions on this model. Haulage was equally impressive, the model proving its capability of handling a 15 carriage train with ease on our test track.

In recent years modellers of BR's Southern Region third-rail electric network have been well served with a raft of Electric Multiple Unit (EMU) releases and this trend continued in September with the arrival of Hornby's 'OO' gauge 2-HAL. While more austere than the 2-BIL EMU before it, this latest two-car unit captured the angular look of the prototype well and featured a wealth of moulded and separate detail.

An eagerly awaited development from Hornby was its Twin Track Sound Digital Command Control (DCC) sound decoders with the first taste of this new technology arriving towards the end of the month, factory installed within its 'OO' gauge BR '8P' 4-6-2 71000 *Duke of Gloucester*. Amongst the 15 onboard sound files were two different whistles, steam exhaust, coasting and wheel slip sounds, coupler clank, doors slamming and even the sound of a sizzling breakfast on the fireman's shovel. Adding approximately £25 to the cost of a standard locomotive, it was a welcome development.

In rolling stock parcels vehicles were the order of the day during September with Hornby's newly tooled 'OO' gauge London and North Eastern Railway (LNER) extra long Covered Carriage Truck (CCT) vans delivered in LNER teak and BR crimson together with Invicta Model Rail's exclusive BR Mk 1 CCT vans commissioned from Bachmann and finished in BR maroon, BR blue, BR Red Star parcels, BR breakdown train yellow and BR Railway Technical Centre (RTC) red and blue liveries.

Hornby's Peppercorn 'K1' 2-6-0 in 'OO'.

October

The month got off to a flying start with Hornby's 'N' gauge 5-BEL Brighton Belle EMU, the first British outline 1:148 scale model to appear in Hornby International's Arnold range. This prestigious five car train lived up to expectations featuring crisply moulded bodies and bogies, correct interiors and working table lamps, plus it ran smoothly too.

Bachmann added two new variants to its popular 'N' gauge Class 37 range of diesel locomotives with the Class 37/4 and Class 37/5 models. Both featured new bodyshells, the 37/4 correctly fitted with central headcode panels and ETH cable boxes while the 37/5 featured the altogether different revised smooth flush cab fronts of the prototypes.

The first 'OO' ready-to-run underground unit – London Transport Museum's Bachmann produced S Stock.

REVIEW OF THE YEAR

Hornby's eagerly awaited Maunsell 'S15' 4-6-0 touched down in September.

Hornby's 'OO' gauge range of BR Mk 1 carriages expanded with the addition of the Second Open (SO) and Tourist Second Open (TSO) carriages. With these latest coaches, Hornby's attention to detail extended to tooling two different interior seating mouldings correctly portraying the 2+1 and 2+2 seat layouts of the real vehicles.

Also during October, a new batch of 'OO' gauge BR Mk 1 horse boxes commissioned by The Model Centre (TMC) arrived. Manufactured by Bachmann exclusively for TMC, these latest vehicles featured strengthening bars on the side doors and/or ends of each vehicle, a development of the prototype while in service. Bachmann also released its 'OO' gauge pipe wagon adding a new open wagon to its »

growing range of steam era wagons.

Heljan's eagerly awaited Class 40 touched down too offering the manufacturer's largest and – in many ways – most impressive locomotive release for 'O' gauge so far. Produced in BR green and BR blue it was a popular seller straight away.

'N' gauge modellers weren't forgotten with new highly detailed rolling stock from Bachmann's Graham Farish range including BR Mk 1 CCT vans and Polybulk covered bogie hopper wagons appearing, the latter featuring some incredibly intricate printing with tri-lingual operating instructions printed on the hopper hood mechanism – in 2mm scale!

November

Leading the way this month was Bachmann's majestic new Stanier 'Duchess' class 'Pacific' 4-6-2 for 'N' gauge. Consigning the previous Graham Farish model to history, this wonderful model certainly looked the part with its high shouldered firebox, wide boiler and long running plate – all looking just so and its performance matched its good looks.

Bachmann also delivered a new version of the Graham Farish 'N' gauge Class 57/3 featuring the distinctive Dellner coupling recessed in the cab front, together with a reworked 'OO' gauge Class 150 two-car Diesel Multiple Unit (DMU).

Heljan's 'OO' gauge Class 05 diesel shunter.

This received modifications to the chassis block, reducing its impact on the interior of the motorised vehicle by two thirds and resulting in a new moulded interior together with interior lighting throughout.

On the rolling stock front Hornby released its 'OO' gauge BR Mk 2e air-conditioned carriages in BR blue and grey and InterCity liveries. Each featured fine tinted flush glazing, neatly moulded body and bogies with three variants produced as a Tourist Standard Open (TSO), Brake Standard Open (BSO) and First Open (FO).

Heljan delivered its 'O' gauge Class 40 – an impressive and heavy weight machine.

December

A nice surprise ahead of Christmas was Hornby's 'OO' Peppercorn 'K1' 2-6-0 which arrived earlier than anticipated, and showed a welcome return to form for the company featuring plenty of separately applied details, decorated cab interior, glazing, fine valve gear, accurate chimney and smooth running mechanism aided by a substantial brass flywheel. It looked good, ran well and proved incredibly popular.

Whilst the prototypes of our next release aren't as popular amongst regular commuters, the arrival of Realtrack Models' long-awaited 'OO' gauge Class 143 two-car 'Pacer' DMU certainly impressed the *Hornby Magazine* team. Our review sample was decorated in the striking First Great Western 'local lines' livery, made up of the many destinations the company serves throughout the West of England. Application of the complex livery was beautifully reproduced in miniature and attention to detail was equally impressive right down to interior handrails picked out in yellow, seat mouldings with grab handles and detailed cab interiors which even featured a moulded fire extinguisher.

New rolling stock this month included Bachmann's delightful new 'N' gauge Graham Farish Midland 20ton brake van and more 'OO' gauge BR Mk 2e carriages from Hornby, the latter featuring factory-fitted interior lighting.

January

The New Year saw Bachmann's long-awaited 'OO' gauge Great Western Railway (GWR) '64XX' 0-6-0PT touch down in the *Hornby Magazine* office. Developed for passenger work first and foremost, this variant of the popular pannier tank captured the look of the prototype well with its wide smokebox door, stepped smokebox saddle and short wheelbase.

Bachmann's new Graham Farish Midland '4F' 0-6-0 set a new standard for 'N' gauge steam locomotives during the month, featuring detailed inside valve gear, hidden coreless motor, an incredibly fine Johnson tender and impeccable performance throughout the speed range on our office test track.

The GWR also benefitted from the arrival of Hornby's new Collett 'Hall' 4-6-0. Designed as a cross range model to suit both the RailRoad and main ranges – much like *Duke of Gloucester* and the 'P2' – the first arrival was 4953 *Pitchford Hall* in the 'Tyseley Connection' train pack with three BR Mk 1 carriages.

Twin Track Sound fitted locomotives continued to arrive from Hornby with the first of its planned diesel models in the form of a Network Rail yellow liveried Class 37 and a BR green Class 40. Both featured an impressive suite of sound files including different horn options, compressor, wheel flange squeal, guard's whistle and much more. They sounded good, ran well and offered an impressive setup for a small premium on the price of a standard diesel locomotive.

New rolling stock included Hornby's recently announced BR 20ton hopper wagon, arriving just weeks after the official unveiling of the Hornby 2015 catalogue range together with the similarly announced LMS horsebox. Meanwhile, newcomer FTG Models delivered its first ready-to-run 'OO' gauge model, a BR SPA air braked plate steel wagon which was well received and plugged another ready-to-run gap.

For 'O' gauge modellers, Heljan's BR Mk 1 57ft General Utility Vans (GUVs) and BR Mk 1 57ft Full Brakes (BG) arrived along with the first of its new air braked wagons, the VBA box van, with our review sample finished in BR late bauxite and featuring crisply moulded panel lines and fine rivet detail on the body sides together with a smooth finish on the unventilated ends.

February

A busy month for releases, Hornby's eagerly-anticipated 'OO' gauge Worsdell 'J15' 0-6-0 »

Kernow Model Rail Centre's Adams 'O2' 0-4-4T for 'OO'.

Dapol's first 'O' gauge ready-to-run locomotive – the Stroudley 'A1' 0-6-0T.

Bachmann's 'N' gauge Bulleid 'Merchant Navy' 4-6-2.

trundled in, delighting us with its top of the range detailing with each model featuring subtle detail differences, superbly decorated cab interiors, twin flywheels and remarkable running characteristics.

Bachmann wasn't to be outdone and released its stunning London, Brighton & South Coast Railway (LBSCR) Billinton 'E4' 0-6-2T, adding another pre grouping locomotive type to the steam roster. Detailing was exemplary and the model even included a set of Southern Railway (SR) headcode discs with slots in the rear for placing over the lamp irons at either end of the model.

Meanwhile, Bachmann's new 'OO' gauge 22ton tube batten wagon also rolled in and impressed with its super-detail touches such as separately fitted metal lamp irons and door stops, while Hornby's upgraded GWR '42XX' 2-8-0T returned to the fold with its new separately fitted smokebox dart and rear guard irons added, which improved the look of the model no end.

It was an expensive month for 'N' gauge modellers too, as Bachmann's Graham Farish range was bolstered by its new 'N' gauge Class 31 diesel locomotive. Surpassing previous models in this scale, the new Class 31 featured crisply moulded communication doors and steps, illuminated headcode boxes, directional lighting, etched roof fan grille and a smooth mechanism. Dapol also re-released its improved 'N' gauge BR 'Britannia' 4-6-2 now with black wheel centres and hexagonal screws on the motion – greatly enhancing its appearance.

Dapol's new 'N' gauge Maunsell carriages impressed with their ornate SR lined olive green livery and new close coupling gangways with Corridor First (FK), Corridor Third (TK),Corridor Brake Third (BTK) and Corridor Composite (CK) variants available together with a delightful Maunsell Van C four wheel parcels luggage van to complete the new line-up. In addition, Southern modellers were also treated to Bachmann's 'N' gauge Graham Farish SR 12ton box vans. They may have been small, but featured plenty of superbly crafted detail.

March

Bachmann's 'OO' gauge GWR 'Modified Hall' returned during March following retooling work to rectify the fire iron tunnel omission on the fireman's side and incorrect steam pipes of the original batch in 2013. This latest release also now featured a new DCC ready chassis which greatly enhanced its performance.

Another returnee was Kernow Model Rail Centre's (KMRC) 'OO' gauge London and South

Amongst the latest Hornby steam locomotives to be released is the GWR's ultimate 4-6-0 – the 'King'.

Western Railway (LSWR) '0298' 2-4-0WT, notable because it was the first ready-to-run model to arrive from DJ Models' manufacturing facility in China. Previously these models had been manufactured by Dapol for KMRC.

Bachmann's newly tooled 'OO' gauge BR 20ton grain hopper wagon rolled in during the month, offering a fine representation of these steel bodied hopper wagons. Meanwhile, 'N' gauge modellers of the contemporary scene were treated to two new modern era wagons from Dapol with the arrival of the IOA and JNA ballast wagons finished in Network Rail's distinctive yellow livery. As expected, they displayed a high level of finesse with finely detailed bodies and underframes.

Heljan didn't disappoint either with more 'O' gauge wagons arriving, expanding its range of ready-to-run vehicles with a set of OAA and OBA air-braked wooden dropside open wagons and 20ton Class B four wheel tanks, in a variety of liveries.

April

The retail arm of the National Railway Museum's (NRM) outpost in Shildon, Locomotion Models, received its exclusive 'OO' gauge Great Northern Railway (GNR) Ivatt 'C1' 4-4-2s during April.

Commissioned from Bachmann for its NRM National Collection in Miniature range, these models arrived slightly later than planned but the wait was certainly worth it. Our review sample of Ivatt 'C1' 251 in original GNR lined green was superbly turned out with its white, black, white lining, detailed and decorated cab interior and GNR pattern tender.

Sussex-based OO Works also unveiled its latest ready-to-run locomotive, the LBSCR 'I3' 4-4-2T, utilising a mix of resin and metal construction. Offering something a little bit different, it featured a flat topped dome, high cab roof and Westinghouse air pump.

Hornby surprised many at the 2014 National Model Railway Exhibition in Birmingham during November when it announced a raft of new products including a set of London, Midland & Scottish Railway (LMS) non corridor stock. Fast forward five months and finished products arrived in the form of Composite, Third and Brake Third carriages, each of our samples being finished in BR crimson. They featured excellent door detail, flush glazed windows, correct pattern roof vents, separately fitted grab rails and fully detailed underframe.

Bachmann continued to delight 'N' gauge modellers with its seemingly endless flow of new products which, during April, included its newly-tooled Graham Farish Bulleid 'Merchant Navy' 4-6-2. Representing one of the final ten BR built locomotives, Bachmann's model captured the characteristic look of the prototype to a tee with its air smoothed body styling and Bulleid-Firth-Brown wheels. Also delivered was the latest variant of the Graham Farish 'N' gauge Class 47, in push-pull fitted Class 47/7 guise displaying its cab front jumper cables and crisply applied BR ScotRail blue-striped livery.

May

May was a fairly quiet month for new releases, but Southern modellers were in for another 'N' gauge treat during the month with the arrival of Bachmann's sublime Maunsell 'N' class 2-6-0. This latest addition to the Graham Farish range displayed great attention to detail and looked the part with its footplate, smoke deflectors and chimney appearing spot on.

Having wowed modellers with its 'OO' gauge versions, Heljan delivered the long-awaited 'O' gauge version of its AC Cars railbus during the month. Weighing in at 1.3kg, this superbly crafted model featured correct corner glass window arrangement, operating headlights, illuminated destination panels and an exquisitely rendered underframe complete with its exposed silver painted fuel tank.

June

Hornby's diminutive LSWR Drummond '700' 0-6-0 added another Southern Region locomotive type to the 'OO' gauge roster. This modest looking locomotive featured a superbly die-cast metal body and captured the distinctive overhang of the prototypes. Impressive dummy inside valve gear was accompanied by a myriad of smokebox fittings, lamp irons, fully detailed cab, sprung metal buffers, guard irons, sandpipes and much more. It all added up to another delightful release from Hornby.

Bachmann's 'OO' gauge Class 43 'Warship' debuted just ahead of the Great Central Railway's Model Event in mid-June. Tooled from scratch, it captured the subtle complex curves and lines of the real locomotives and featured plenty of small details which even included tiny lifting hooks for the roof – each of which required fitting by the customer, but enhanced the look of the model even further.

DCC sound continued to drive sales with Hornby's new Twin Track Sound (TTS) models making sound more affordable. June saw the arrival of the company's latest TTS fitted models in the Railroad range including London and North Eastern Railway (LNER) 'A1' 4-6-2 4472 *Flying Scotsman* and Class 47/4 47402 in BR 'large logo' livery. Both offered plenty of exciting play value: the sound decoder in the 'A1' featured an impressive 17 different sound functions including three different whistles while the Class 47 diesel locomotive included 24 sound functions with manual notching of the engine sounds possible too.

Hornby's super-detailed range of quality carriages was also bolstered with the release of the first K-Type all-steel Pullman vehicles. Five vehicles formed the new range including a Parlour Brake Third, Kitchen First, Parlour First, Kitchen Third and Parlour Third. Each offered finely detailed panels, separately fitted handrails, working table lamps, full underframe detail, flush glazing and were »

The all new Stanier 'Duchess' for 'N' gauge by Bachmann.

Hornby's 2-HAL EMU for 'OO'.

Bachmann's 'OO' gauge BR 22ton Tube wagon.

Hornby's fully detailed LNER Gresley 'P2' 2-8-2 for 'OO'.

superbly decorated with intricate gold lining, Pullman legends and crests. Truly worthy of the Pullman name.

For 'N' gauge modellers, another rolling stock gap was filled with the arrival of the Graham Farish Southern Bogie B Van from Bachmann. Our impressive review sample was finished in BR green and featured grey roof and black underframe with black ends. Bodyside planking was intricately moulded, as were the metal support straps and doors. Even the glazing featured printed meshing.

July

Representing its first all new locomotive in almost two years, Dapol's 'N' gauge GWR 'Grange' 4-6-0 proved to be well turned-out. It filled a useful gap in the range of 'N' gauge GWR designed motive power, with its improved paint finish, etched metal name and numberplates, copper clad chimney and brass safety valve bonnet.

Heljan completed its 'OO' Railbus trilogy with the release of the Park Royal Railbus. Correctly proportioned windows, finely moulded seat back handrails and illuminated destination panels were just some of the standout features on this impressive new incarnation of the diminutive model.

Following a surprise announcement the previous month, July saw the arrival of an advance batch of London Transport Museum's (LTM) specially commissioned 'OO' gauge models of the London Underground S Stock. Manufactured by Bachmann and exclusive to the LTM, these sub surface EMUs were released in a four-car train pack comprising two motorised driving cars and two trailer cars together with additional vehicles available separately to make up prototypical seven or eight car sets. Each unit was fitted with directional lighting, 21-pin DCC decoder sockets in each motor car and featured a new low profile motor that could offer new opportunities for the manufacturer in the future.

Heljan's long-awaited Hunslet 0-6-0 diesel shunters also appeared during the month and featured a high level of detail including operational electric marker lights, fine mesh behind the radiator slats, crisply moulded Hunslet name badge, fine coupling rods, scale wheels and crisply printed BR wasp stripes at each end. The Danish manufacturer's attention to detail also extended to featuring the correct cab window shape for these Eastern Region variants.

A delightful set of Hawksworth coaches was also added to Bachmann's Graham Farish 'N' gauge range during the month with the arrival of a Corridor Second (SK), Corridor Composite (CK), Corridor Brake Second (BSK) and Full Brake (BG) finished in BR carmine and cream. Body, roof and underframe detailing was exquisite and each featured correct window arrangements and fine moulding of all components, raising the bar for rolling stock in this scale once again.

Modelling London Underground operations became a possibility with the arrival of Heljan's Metropolitan Railway Bo-Bo electric.

The 'Brighton Belle' EMU for 'N' gauge – Hornby's first ready-to-run British outline 'N' gauge model.

August

Having only been announced the previous December, Hornby's 'OO' gauge Maunsell 'S15' 4-6-0 was presented for review during August. This stunning new locomotive featured a new version of the SR bogie tender with straight sides and was decorated in a semi-satin BR black paint finish with red bufferbeams and brass pipework. Its performance was equally outstanding, hauling a 25 wagon goods train around our office test track without hesitation.

Hornby also delivered the first of its 'OO' gauge Railroad BR Crosti boilered '9F' 2-10-0 locomotives. The model featured an impressive body with separately fitted handrails, superbly moulded pipework, side exhaust, metal buffers and glazed cab interior. The later version with offside smoke deflector followed shortly after. Whilst perhaps not up to the high specification of recent offerings from Hornby, this model does sit in the RailRoad range and provides a great basis for further detailing.

Kernow Model Rail Centre's new 'OO' gauge LSWR Adams 'O2' 0-4-4T arrived towards the end of the month, four years after it was first announced. Representing the first fully completed model from KMRC's manufacturing partner DJ Models, this latest arrival bristled with detail and ran incredibly smoothly, even including pre-wired connectors for DCC sound installations.

With a few delays along the way, Bachmann's newly-tooled 'N' gauge Peppercorn 'A2' 4-6-2 arrived for review during the month. The wait had definitely been worth it, with Bachmann capturing the different wheel diameter, wheelbase and length correctly from the 'A1'. The body moulding looked just so as did the electric lamps, lamp irons, boiler fittings and more. Performance was equally impressive.

A simple but important item of rolling stock arrived in August in the form of Bachmann's 'OO' gauge SR Passenger Luggage Van (PLV)/Parcels and Miscellaneous Vans (PMV), a common type of parcels vehicle seen throughout the rail network. Bachmann's new models reflected the variations in body styles and colours and captured the looks of the prototype well.

Given their die-cast model pedigree, Oxford Rail had a lot to live up to following the announcement of its new range of model railway products. The first of these new products arrived during the month in the form of three 'OO' gauge 12ton private owner open mineral wagons. Commendably fine, they featured crisp planking, strapping and bolt head detail together with metal headed buffers, fine handbrake levers, end door swivel bar, coupling hooks and finely moulded interior discharge doors. A good start for the fledgling brand.

September

September was a busy month for Hornby with the appearance of its glamorous new 'OO' gauge GWR Collett 'King' 4-6-0. Detailed thoroughly from front to back, the model featured correct pattern GWR lamp brackets, separately fitted smokebox dart, pipework, lubricator boxes, copper capped chimney, handrails, running plate conduit, fully detailed and decorated cab interior and more. It also performed impeccably and hauled 12 carriages on our test track with ease.

Hornby's Great Eastern Railway (GER) 'D16/3' 4-4-0 for 'OO' also docked in September. Representing the Gresley rebuild of the

Heljan's 'O' gauge AC Cars railbus.

Realtrack Models impressively finished 'OO' Class 143 DMU.

# Rolling stock highlights

Oxford Rail's first ready-to-run wagons – the RCH seven-plank in 'OO'.

Heljan 'O' gauge BR Mk 1 GUV van.

Dapol 'N' gauge Maunsell Brake Third.

locomotives. It featured the distinctive round topped firebox of the prototype, neatly moulded boiler pipework, guard irons, sprung metal buffers, removable coal load and detail differences between models. Despite its short wheelbase, the 'D16/3' also proved how sure footed it was thanks to a die-cast metal boiler and not a traction tyre in sight, hauling eight carriages with ease during our tests.

Hornby also delivered a new version of its delightful Sentinel 0-4-0 diesel shunter fitted with outside coupling rods for the first time. Like its predecessor, its performance was also impeccable.

Much focus has been placed on London Underground's routes this year and, at the beginning of September, Heljan delivered its latest model of the Metropolitan Railway Bo-Bo electric locomotives. Our review sample was finished as No. 8 *Sherlock Holmes* in the simplified post war London Transport livery which looked superb and performed just as well.

Rails of Sheffield received its original condition models of LMS diesel prototypes 10000 and 10001. Commissioned by Bachmann and produced as a limited edition our sample was presented in a wooden box and featured 10000 in original black with LMS lettering and 10001 in BR black without lettering. Both exhibited astonishing attention to detail with many variations between the two locomotives being modelled.

Dapol's first ready-to-run locomotive for 'O' gauge, the LBSCR Stroudley 'Terrier' 0-6-0T, finally appeared during September. It had been a long time in development but the wait was certainly worth it, the eye-catching model certainly looking the part. Featuring a detailed plastic body, heavy metal chassis and powerful can motor it also featured tiny flickering red LEDs in the firebox within the cab which was a neat touch.

Finally, Bachmann's newly tooled 'OO' gauge Hawksworth designed BR autotrailer rolled in. Available in BR carmine and cream, BR crimson and BR maroon liveries, this useful vehicle captured the look of the prototype well with its angular cab, large windows, retractable steps and distinctive warning gong above the cab.

The 'J15' 0-6-0 from Hornby in 'OO'.

www.hornbymagazine.com

REVIEW OF THE YEAR

Hornby BR 20ton hopper for 'OO'.

'O' gauge VBA van from Heljan.

Hawksworth Corridor Second in 'N' gauge by Bachmann.

The year ahead

What a year it has turned out to be with a constant throughput of stunning models in 'N', 'OO' and 'O'. For me, Heljan's 'O' gauge AC Cars railbus was a personal favourite - and who would have thought this time last year that we would have a 'OO' gauge model of the latest London Underground S Stock available now?

Hornby's budget DCC sound fitted models were undoubtedly another highlight and the good news appears to be that many of the manufacturer's supply chain issues are easing now. Retailer commissions continue to be popular with Kernow and Hattons working hard to deliver their promised lines of locomotives and rolling stock.

With new manufacturers entering the market and a stellar line-up of new projects in the offing the future certainly looks bright for the hobby, and there will no doubt be more surprises to come.

Rest assured we'll be here to report on progress.

For more on future locomotive releases see Forward to 2016 on pages 120-127. ■

All-steel K Type Pullman brake for 'OO' by Hornby.

Invicta Model Rail's Bachmann produced BR Mk 1 CCT van in 'OO'.

Hornby's LNER extra-long CCT for 'OO'.

Bachmann 'N' gauge Polybulk.

REALITY CHECK

THE BR TYPE 4 DIESELS

Perhaps the most successful group of diesel locomotives introduced in the modernisation years were the versatile Type 4s, some of which are still around today many years since they were first brought into service, as **EVAN GREEN-HUGHES** describes.

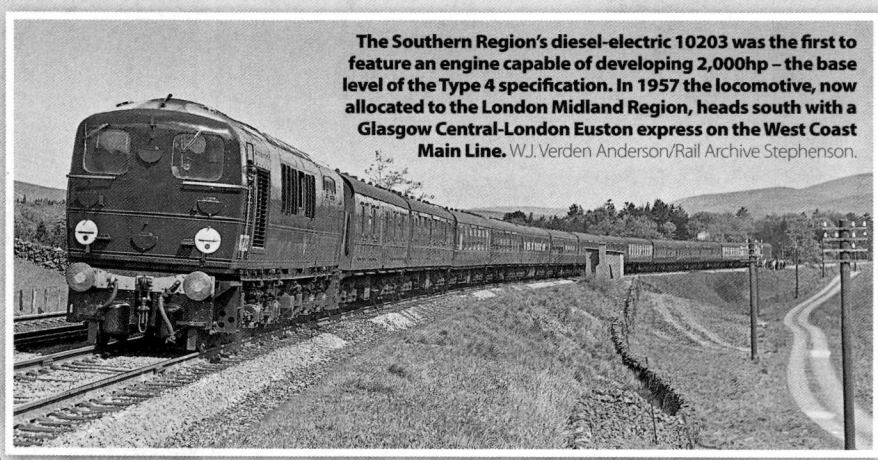

The Southern Region's diesel-electric 10203 was the first to feature an engine capable of developing 2,000hp – the base level of the Type 4 specification. In 1957 the locomotive, now allocated to the London Midland Region, heads south with a Glasgow Central-London Euston express on the West Coast Main Line. W.J. Verden Anderson/Rail Archive Stephenson.

English Electric's first production Type 4 diesels were the Class 40s which weighed in at 133tons and had eight axles. D239 climbs Cockburnspath bank with the Up 'Heart of Midlothian' on June 13 1961. Hugh Harman/Rail Archive Stephenson.

REALITY CHECK

FOR MORE THAN 50 years in the latter half of the 20th century a visit to a station almost anywhere in the country was sure to produce the sight of one of the numerous Type 4 diesels. These locomotives were used on anything from crack expresses to humble local freight trains and were so successful that at one time more than 1,000 were in service. One type, the Class 47, numbered no less than 512 examples and some of these still survive on the network although these days they are mainly used for special trains and for 'one off' duties rather than in front line service.

The designation of Type 4, or Type C as they were originally known, was given to locomotives of between 2,000 and 2,999hp which puts the most powerful examples on a par with the most powerful steam locomotives at the time. Interestingly when the Type 4 was specified in the early 1950s no one had actually produced a locomotive in this country powerful enough to fit into this category: in fact the figure of 2,000hp was chosen because that was the limit of what was thought to be available from contemporary power units.

At that time practical experience was limited to five locomotives, two of which had been ordered by the London Midland & Scottish Railway (LMS) and, as 10000 and 10001, had put in some very good performances. These two only developed around 1,600hp each and had to be used double headed when allocated to hauling heavy and fast express trains.

The Southern had been responsible for building three locomotives with roughly similar power plants to the LMS twins but these were carried on massive eight wheel bogies to reduce the axle load. The first two of these were rated at 1,700hp but the final one, 10203 - which came along in 1954 some three years after the others - had the Mk II version of the English Electric 16SVT engine which produced 2,000hp. At last this meant that there was a diesel engine available that was capable of doing the work of the larger steam classes, making it comparable with mixed traffic designs such as the Gresley 'V2' 2-6-2 or the Stanier 'Jubilee' 4-6-0.

At the end of 1954 the British Transport Commission accepted a recommendation that 174 diesel locomotives should be purchased of various types and that these should be subject to a three-year evaluation programme before mass production commenced. Amongst these were a number of competing designs in the Type 4 category, intended to undertake the heaviest and most arduous duties. Tender documents were sent out and more than 200 »

The last Type 4s to be built were the English Electric Class 50s for working north of Crewe on the West Coast Main Line. On May 20 1969 D422 waits to leave Carlisle with the 3.09pm to London Euston. Bob Tuck/Rail Archive Stephenson.

The Brush Class 47 became BR's standard Type 4 and worked across the system. D1714 stands at London Paddington after arrival with an express from Birkenhead on April 7 1964. *Brian Stephenson*

BRCW's Type 4 prototype D0260 Lion *was an impressive machine in its striking white livery. On May 17 1962* Lion *passes High Wycombe with the 12.10pm London Paddington-Birkenhead Woodside express.* Hugh Harman/Rail Archive Stephenson.

proposals were received in return, giving the BR Board a major headache in sorting out which were likely to be best.

An English Electric start

One of the leading contenders was English Electric as that company had already proved that it could provide the equipment for a fully-functioning locomotive. However, there was general dissatisfaction with the two existing designs, neither of which entirely ticked all the boxes required. In consequence plans were drawn up to produce a locomotive that was to all intents and purposes an amalgamation of the existing designs.

The mechanical layout was very similar to the Southern Region's 10203 and the design incorporated the same ponderous eight-wheel 1-Co-Co-1 bogies in order to reduce axle weight. However above the bogies the styling used incorporated the prominent nose that was commonly used on English Electric products and which had appeared on 10000/10001 rather than the flat front used on 10201-10203. What emerged was eventually to be known as the Class 40 and extended to 200 examples.

The first of these, D200, was delivered to Stratford in March 1958 and made its first run to Norwich on April 18. On that route it was used instead of a 'Britannia' steam locomotive but it failed to show any superiority over the Class 7 'Pacific', though it was a match in terms of availability between maintenance. Subsequently concerns were expressed at the highest level about the performance of the new diesels and this resulted in the Eastern Region refusing the type as replacements for its crack 'Pacifics' on the East Coast Main Line. As the first Type 4s were no more powerful than its 'A1', 'A3' and 'A4' steam locomotives this made sense.

Clearly more power would be needed but plans to uprate the English Electric engine came to nothing and subsequent locomotives were built to the original specification. In May 1959 the London Midland Region began to receive the EE Type 4 and before long they were being used to displace Stanier 'Pacifics' on the West Coast Main Line with some success – although there was little if any improvement in performance over the steam powered 'Pacifics'. The Class 40s also proved themselves to be very competent freight engines, with their massive 133tons deadweight being a distinct advantage when hauling a string of unfitted wagons

'Peak' performance

British Railways Derby Works produced a design for a very similar locomotive, though this time using a Sulzer power unit, but this did »

The 'Western' hydraulics allowed the end of steam on the Western Region as they provided enough power to out-perform the GWR 'King' 4-6-0s. D1000 Western Enterprise *arrives at Ruabon with the 1.10pm London Paddington-Birkenhead Woodside on July 23 1963.* Brian Stephenson.

not appear for almost a year after the English Electric product. By this time 2,300hp was available and the resulting engine was billed as the most powerful to be owned by British Railways up until that time.

Again the bogie design was based on that used on 10203, while the styling included the English Electric style body with prominent nose. The first of these was numbered D1 and named *Scafell Pike* and the nine that followed were also named after prominent hills, thus gaining the class the collective name of 'Peaks'. This initial batch was sent to Camden, but soon graduated to main line services out of Euston and St Pancras. As with the English Electric product, they were soon rated as inadequately powered for much of what they were called upon to do.

Initially the 'Peaks' were less reliable than the Class 40s and there had to be a number of minor modifications to try and improve performance. By this time an order had been placed for a further 137 of the design and later in the year this was followed by another 64 but this time with Brush rather than Crompton Parkinson electrical gear meaning that there were many more locomotives to follow on from what was basically an unsatisfactory design. At this point Sulzer brought out its 'B' series power unit rated at 2,500hp and so this was fitted to all 'Peaks' from D11 onwards.

With this upgrade and a number of technical modifications the class settled down to become reliable and sturdy workhorses. They became synonymous with the Midland Main Line between St Pancras and Sheffield, along with the onward routes to Manchester and Carlisle and were also later used on Newcastle to Liverpool duties. However long-term reliability was never as good as the English Electric product despite over 200 modifications being made to them during the 1960s.

The hydraulic experiment
One of the biggest problems with the English Electric and Sulzer Type 4s was that they used a considerable amount of power to shift their own massive weight around. In other countries designers had used integral body construction with lighter high-revving diesel engines coupled to hydraulic transmissions to overcome this problem and this was of interest to British Railways officials - so much so that a fact finding visit had been made to Germany to see such locomotives in action.

In the UK the North British Locomotive Company had a licence to manufacture German Voith hydraulic transmissions and MAN diesel engines and subsequently that company was given an order to build five 2,000hp Type 4s for comparison purposes. Unfortunately these locomotives were constructed using traditional techniques and when completed weighed 117tons, only 16tons lighter than a Class 40. Part of the reason for this was that the original specification called for a truly mixed traffic locomotive capable of working unfitted freight and thus some degree of weight was

Sulzer's first Type 4s were the 'Peak' series which later became classes 44, 45 and 46. Class 45 D27 passes Peartree with the Up 'Devonian' on April 18 1964.
Gordon Hepburn/Rail Archive Stephenson.

required for brake force purposes.

The first of this class, D600 *Active*, was actually in service four months before the first Class 40 but it and its four sisters were destined to be a one-off order as there was general dissatisfaction with the performance and layout.

It was, however, felt that there was room for development and as a result the former Great Western Railway works at Swindon set about designing a new Type 4 diesel-hydraulic, using as a basis the German V200 which was a revolutionary locomotive which incorporated a stress-bearing body that enabled the withdrawal of a conventional heavy chassis.

What resulted was a twin-engined machine of similar power to the Class 40s and 'Peaks' but which weighed a staggering 55tons less. This lack of weight was a significant issue when working freight trains but it was then thought that this could be overcome by fitting such trains with continuous brakes. So successful were these 'Warships' that 71 were

Pilot Scheme 'Peak' D7 *Ingleborough* leads an Up coal train near Newton Harcourt on a misty November 18 1967. Brian Stephenson

eventually built, with the power uprated to 2,270hp. These were supplied by Swindon works and by North British with some being fitted with Maybach engines and others NBL-MAN versions. The 'Warships' soon became firm fixtures of the Western Region's express services but never achieved the reliability of their diesel-electric cousins.

However good the 'Warships' were, just like their diesel-electric equivalents they were not a match for that ultimate development of Great Western steam engines, the Collett 'King' 4-6-0, and so that steam could be replaced on the fastest services Swindon drew up a larger diesel-hydraulic class, which were to become known as the 'Westerns'. These were six axle machines fitted with two Maybach MD655 engines and developing 2,700hp but yet still only weighing 108tons.

They largely followed the design of the 'Warships' but their external appearance was heavily influenced by British Railways' design panel, meaning that what emerged was perhaps one of the most handsome diesels ever made. The fleet was built at Crewe as well as Swindon. The 'Westerns' handled prestige expresses on the Western Region as well as other fast traffic but were usually regarded as express locomotives, rather than as general purpose as with many of the other Type 4 designs.

The new generation

While the Western Region had settled on the 'Warships' and 'Westerns' for its requirements elsewhere there was general dissatisfaction with the diesel-electric Type 4s on offer. A lighter but more powerful locomotive was required and this led to an outline specification being drawn up in 1960.

At this time there were three major locomotive manufacturers very keen to get future orders and each one constructed at their own expense a prototype for trials. Birmingham Railway Carriage and Wagon Co (BRCW) came up with *Lion*, a stunning all-white Sulzer-engined Co-Co of 2,750hp and weighing 114tons; Brush provided *Falcon*, equipped with two high-speed Maybach engines and providing 2,880hp for 115tons while the final contender was DP2, which »

looked very much like a 'Deltic' but which was fitted with a single English Electric engine providing 2,700hp for a weight of 105tons.

Of the three *Lion* seemed to offer the best package but unfortunately its maker, BRCW, was in a parlous financial state and there was serious doubt that it would be able to provide the locomotives required. *Falcon* was also a fine piece of work but the twin engine arrangement was not favoured and so Brush was set the task of preparing a second design which was in effect a simplified version of *Lion* built on the principles of *Falcon*.

The new locomotives were to use the electrical gear and engines which had been ordered for a final batch of 'Peaks' but these were to be fitted into a bodyshell in which some of the strength was derived from the body construction itself, allowing a reduction in overall weight. What emerged from this exercise was a locomotive that was to be an outstanding success and which was to become known in every corner of the country as the Brush Type 4 and later Class 47.

Even before the first of the new design had made an appearance British Railways was placing orders for more, with construction being undertaken not only by Brush at Loughborough but also by British Railways itself at Crewe Works. The design offered 2,750hp from a Sulzer engine for an overall weight of 112tons, around 750hp more than a Class 40 for a reduction in weight of almost 20 tons. Following experience with the pilot batch, the order book quickly reached 270 and it was extended to 512 over the following years. Most of these were equipped for steam train heating, although 81 were built specifically for freight work and had no heating capability. In addition as built the first 20 plus D1702-D1706 were equipped for electric train heating but many of the others were fitted with this equipment in later years.

The Class 47 soon settled down to become one of the principal locomotives of the modernisation era and proved equally at home on express passenger trains as well as goods. Many replaced Class 40s and 'Peaks' which were then cascaded to lesser duties while others took over duties previously worked by larger steam engines and which had proved unsuitable for earlier diesel types.

Last of the breed

With the development of a numerous and successful design like the Class 47 it is a little surprising that when British Railways was seeking a Type 4 locomotive for the modernisation of the northern half of the West Coast Main Line that a further Type 4 should have been developed. The introduction of the fleet of 50 Class 50s came about because by the time they were required in 1965 there were numerous teething troubles with Class 47s and it was felt that a more reliable locomotive could be produced.

Using their prototype DP2 as a base English Electric calculated that a reliability figure of 84% could be achieved with a new design and promised that 42 locomotives a day would be available for service if it was awarded a contract to supply a new design.

However the Class 50s were not just to be a production run of DP2s for by this time British Railways had become image conscious and the class was expected to comply with the design panel's flat fronted design as used on the Class 47. In addition air and vacuum train braking was required, along with electric train heating equipment. The locomotives also featured more

BRITISH RAILWAYS TYPE 4 DIESEL LOCOMOTIVES							
BUILDER	CLASS	BUILT	NO. BUILT	WHEEL ARRANGEMENT	POWER	WEIGHT	LENGTH
English Electric	40	1958-1962	200	1-Co-Co-1	2,000hp	133tons	69ft 6in
North British	41	1958-1959	5	A1A-A1A	2,000hp	117tons	65ft 0in
BR Swindon	42	1958-1961	38	B-B	2,270hp	78tons	60ft 0in
North British	43	1960-1962	33	B-B	2,200hp	79tons	60ft 0in
BR Derby	44	1959-1960	10	1-Co-Co-1	2,300hp	133tons	67ft 11in
BR Derby/Crewe	45	1960-1962	127	1-Co-Co-1	2,500hp	136tons	67ft 11in
BR Derby	46	1961-1963	56	1-Co-Co-1	2,500hp	138tons	67ft 11in
Brush/BR Crewe	47	1962-1968	512	Co-Co	2,580hp	112tons	63ft 7in
Brush	48	1966	5	Co-Co	2,650hp	112tons	63ft 7in
English Electric	50	1967-1968	50	Co-Co	2,750hp	115tons	68ft 6in
BR Swindon/Crewe	52	1961-1964	74	C-C	2,700hp	108tons	68ft 0in

Experimental Brush Co-Co D0280 *Falcon* **arrives at London King's Cross with the 'Master Cutler' Pullman train from Sheffield on June 18 1962.** Brian Stephenson.

The Western Region's production 'Warships' were revolutionary for the use of a stress bearing body which helped reduce the weight of these twin-engined high revving diesel hydraulics. D853 *Thurster* **has just passed Hayes & Harlington with the 1.45pm London Paddington-Weston-super-Mare on October 19 1963.** Brian Stephenson.

electronics than had been used on previous designs. Prototype locomotive D400 arrived in Crewe for tests in September 1967 and was accepted into traffic that October with the class soon taking over work on principal expresses to the North from Crewe, sometimes working in pairs. Once the line from Crewe to Scotland was electrified the class was transferred to the Western Region where they helped displace diesel-hydraulic Type 4s.

The Class 50s were the final Type 4s to enter service with British Rail. From the early 1970s there had been a realisation that the days of the general purpose locomotives were numbered. For freight work more powerful locomotives were required that would enable the length of block trains to be increased while for passenger duties thoughts were turning towards high-powered fixed-formation trains, including the High Speed Train (HST).

The Western Region soon lost its Type 4 diesel-hydraulics in favour of diesel-electrics transferred in from other regions to increase on standardisation. The 'Warships' began to be taken out of service from 1968 and all had gone by 1971 while the 'Westerns' had all gone by 1978. Introduction of the HST enabled Class 47s to be cascaded to other duties and this in turn meant that the way was clear for the withdrawal of some of the earlier Type 4s.

The Class 40s were by this time considered to be underpowered and they were taken out of service between 1976 and 1985 with one dominant factor being that they were not fitted with electric train heating equipment and could not be upgraded without making significant reductions in the power available for hauling trains. Many did not survive long enough to be fitted with train air brake equipment and retained only vacuum equipment until the end.

Withdrawal of most of the 'Peaks' took place at around the same time, although the last one was not taken out of service until 1989. Many of these had been equipped for electric train heating and were allocated to the Midland Main Line, or to Trans Pennine duties.

The Class 47s survived relatively intact and underwent a number of upgrades. Many were fitted with electric train heating equipment and almost all were dual braked so that they could be used with air braked rolling stock. Some were fitted with long-range fuel tanks while others received push-pull equipment so that they could be operated with Driving Van Trailers on the route between Edinburgh and Glasgow. However the introduction of Class 220/221 'Voyager' units to Cross-Country services saw many examples laid aside in the early 2000s while a decade earlier Class 158 DMUs took over duties such as Trans-Pennine passenger services. The Class 50s were similarly replaced by units on services to the South West.

The last survivors

Today there is little traditional work left for the Type 4. Smaller operators such as West Coast Railways, Colas and Direct Rail Services still use the Class 47 in penny numbers for charter or specialised freight duties while some Class 47s have been used as the basis for conversion to the more powerful Class 57, which uses a General Motors engine and upgraded traction equipment in the old bodyshell. These were developed by Freightliner and a later electric train heating equipped version is used on the 'Night Riviera' 'sleeper' train from Paddington to Penzance. The Class 57/3s ordered by Virgin Trains for rescue duties on the West Coast Main Line and hauling Class 390 Electric Multiple Units from Crewe to Holyhead have been transferred to other smaller operators.

The Type 4 was once seen as a high-powered maid of all work which could take on almost any duty asked of it and the specification proved successful for many years. That very few are active today is merely a sign that traffic requirements have moved on to faster and heavier things, rather than of any basic flaw in the original specification. ∎

> *"The Type 4 was once seen as a high-powered maid of all work for almost any duty."*
> **EVAN GREEN-HUGHES**

Rolling stock and operation

Creating the roster for West Riding Power has been an enjoyable task with its early 1980s theme. **MIKE WILD** reviews the project, its rolling stock and how it operates.

ON THE FACE OF IT THE 1980s might not seem like the most interesting of railway periods. BR blue prevailed as the primary colour of the locomotives and rolling stock, but from the middle of the decade a new wave of liveries started to appear with the rise of 'large logo' blue and Railfreight's 'red stripe' colour scheme.

But it wasn't just colour where change was coming. The way goods was transported was developing too and while steam era vacuum braked goods stock was still an everyday sight in the first few years of the 1980s modern air braked goods wagons were on the rise. Express passenger traffic had already been revitalised by air-conditioned Mk 2 and Mk 3 carriages, but they were operating side by side with the Mk 1 stock too. Long distance trains were increasingly in the hands of BR's impressive High Speed Trains (HSTs) which dominated on the East Coast, Great Western and Midland Main Lines.

The second half of the decade witnessed even greater change with the arrival of the second generation of Diesel Multiple Units (DMUs) which like a tide eradicated locomotive hauled passenger services on routes such as the Trans-Pennine lines from Manchester into the West Riding to Leeds and beyond. BR's freight sector took on a brand new look when it was sectorised as Trainload Freight to feature a triple grey livery with branding for coal, petroleum, construction, distribution, metals and general traffics. None of this happened overnight though and even into the 1990s BR's corporate blue colour scheme remained an everyday part of the railway scene.

With so much change, identifying a time period – and without straying from it – has been something of a challenge in creating West Riding Power's roster. The initial idea was to cover the period from 1978 to 1986, but there is so much temptation to move

Merry-go-round traffic was intensive in the West Riding. A Class 56 passes by on the main line with empty HAA hoppers as a pair of Class 20s approach the power station in the background.

WEST RIDING POWER – THE FLEET

CLASS	LIVERY	MANUFACTURER	DCC ADDRESS
Class 08	BR blue	Bachmann	n/a
Class 20 20063	BR blue	Bachmann	2063
Class 20 20132	BR Railfreight grey	Bachmann	2032
Class 24 24035	BR blue	Bachmann	2435
Class 25 25231	BR blue	Bachmann	2531
Class 31 31173	BR blue	Bachmann	3173
Class 37 37027	BR 'large logo' blue	Bachmann	3727
Class 37 37054	BR blue	Bachmann	3754
Class 37 37238	BR blue	Bachmann	3738
Class 46 46053	BR blue	Bachmann	4653
Class 47 47404	BR blue	Bachmann	4704
Class 47 47535	BR 'large logo' blue	Bachmann	4735
Class 56 56070	BR blue	Dapol	5670
Class 56 56090	BR 'large logo' blue	Dapol	5690
Class 58 58012	BR Railfreight grey	Dapol	5812
Class 101, two car	BR blue	Bachmann	1012
Class 101, three car	BR blue	Bachmann	1013
Class 108, two car	BR blue	Bachmann	1082
Class 253 253023	BR blue	Dapol	0253

A pair of Class 20s enter West Riding power station loop with a rake of MGR hoppers as a Class 56 passes in the opposite direction with another coal train.

The early 1980s still played host to early diesel classes including Class 25s. Here a '25' takes a Speedlink train across the truss bridge while in the background a Class 56 moves through the discharge shed at the power station.

forward and starting bringing together train formations from the late 1980s with coal and metal sector liveried locomotives sneaking in. We're aiming to stick with the original plan, but don't be surprised if you see a few trains from the final years of the 1980s running when the layout is on show.

Happily ready-to-run stock in 'N' gauge has moved on leaps and bounds both in quality and quantity when it comes to the period in question. BR blue locomotives and rolling stock are well catered for and we've enjoyed building upon a collection which started a few years ago when the first ideas for a BR blue period layout were drawn up.

The roster

Developing the locomotive roster for West Riding Power started with searching for images on the internet from the period in question. Looking back at the late 1970s and early 1980s it showed a railway in change. Locomotives from the 1950s and early 1960s were running side by side with new additions such as the Class 56 heavy freight diesels and the supremely successful HSTs. Local traffic was in the hands of rattling DMUs while locomotive hauled passenger trains were still an everyday part of operations.

We wanted to represent all of this and through the impressive selection of ready-to-run locomotives produced by Bachmann in its Graham Farish range and Dapol we had an ample choice. Some classes were more common than others in the West Riding, but others weren't. Classes 20, 24 and 58 were rare visitors to the area in question whereas classes 25, 37, 47, 45 and 56 formed the bulk of the motive power fleet for the West Riding. Nevertheless, we've set out to model all of these partly for interest and partly for personal choice – we couldn't resist a pair of Class 20s on a coal train and equally nor did we want to run the layout without a Railfreight 'red stripe' Class 58.

All of the locomotives have been fitted with 6-pin Digital Command Control (DCC) decoders using Bachmann 36-558A decoders for Bachmann locomotives and Gaugemaster DCC23 decoders for Dapol models. These are simple plug and play decoders which take a matter of minutes to install – the only complications are the Diesel Multiple Units (DMUs) which are more difficult to dismantle. All of the locomotives, except the Class 46, feature directional lighting and this is controlled by function 0 on the DCC handset.

To enhance the appearance of the locomotives the front couplings have been removed from all locomotives and the supplied bufferbeam details have been fitted. This gives the models a much more realistic appearance. Superglue is used to fix these details in place and while some are very fiddly to install they are well worth the effort.

With West Riding Power being a brand new layout a campaign of weathering is underway for the fleet. So far only a handful have been completed, but others are in works to bring them up to standard and create a continuity for the appearance of the layout. Weathering has involved the use of Lifecolor acrylics airbrushed onto models as well as the highly useful Adam Wilder Nitro Line washes which have really helped to bring life to locomotives.

Viewed from above the power station complex arrangement is clear. A Class 56 works through the discharge shed.

Addressing

An important consideration with any DCC controlled layout is how the locomotives will be addressed. An addressing system needs to be simple to remember and easy to use, especially if you intend on having multi-operator sessions.

In the past we've used sequence numbering for locomotives – 0001, 0002, 0003, 0004 etc. – but once you have more than four or five locomotives it becomes very difficult to clearly remember which one is which. For our steam era layouts we've adopted a system based on using the last four digits from each locomotive identity which works in 99% of all cases and is a logical means of identifying different engines for a DCC system. For one thing, we can never forget an address!

> *"All the locomotives have been fitted with 6-pin Digital Command Control decoders."*
>
> **MIKE WILD**

West Riding Power uses an adapted version of this system. Rather than using the last four digits because all locomotives have TOPS class number – 20, 24, 37 and so on – we have used the first two and the last two numbers from each locomotive number to create the address. For example Class 20 20063 is address 2063 and Class 31 31173 is address 3173. This way operators only have to read the last two digits of a locomotive's number to recognise its address as the first two will always be its class number.

There are exceptions to the rule, primarily for multiple units where they either have no set number or have a six figure address. In this case units are numbered by the classification and the number of vehicles in the consist. For example a two-car Class 101 is

WEST RIDING POWER

Carrying 'large logo' blue livery and representing the mid 1980s, a Class 56 enters the power station with a rake of MGR hoppers for unloading. The cooling towers dominate the skyline.

address 1012, a three-car Class 101 is address 1013 and a two-car Class 108 DMU is 1082. This same system has been used for all our DMU models across all layouts, but as none will operate on the same layout at the same time it won't cause problems.

Another special case – there will always be locomotives which don't fit into a standard protocol – is the HST set which, as there is only one of it, has been given address 0253 reflecting the fact that, in the period in question, the sets were numbered as Class 253s.

Rolling stock

The passenger and goods fleet for West Riding Power has been interesting to assemble. It is quite surprising how much steam era goods stock was still running into the 1980s with the last vacuum braked trains being withdrawn from service in the 1990s. This is something that we are looking to represent with the layout which will feature trains varying from mixed formations including vacuum braked wagons through to modern air braked stock including cargo wagons, cement and steel wagons.

One of the principal freight flows to be modelled is coal traffic. This is taken care of by a rake of Graham Farish HAA hoppers and it is planned that a second rake will be added to the stock list in the future. Joining these are block trains of 100ton bogie TEA tankers, a Freightliner train and a mixed rake of stock forming a trip freight. The latter can be broken down into shorter trains – it wasn't uncommon in the period to see single wagon freights.

Representing earlier wagons is being done carefully, but the roster includes a set of 22ton Presflo cement wagons, a rake of 20ton hoppers and a handful of box vans in BR bauxite. Further freight formations will follow and it is planned to develop a block steel working formed of BDA bogie bolster wagons.

The passenger fleet initially concentrates on three types of train: DMUs of classes 101 and 108 for stopping trains, locomotive hauled rakes of Mk 1/Mk 2 stock for Trans Pennine services and a HST set to represent a diverted East Coast Main Line working. There is plenty of room for this area of the stock to develop in the future and it may be that we look to model the last years of 'Deltic' operation at the early end of the layout's time period.

There is also a plan to investigate putting together a stock set to operate West Riding Power in the 1985-1990 timeframe allowing

Vacuum braked goods trains were still a daily sight in the early 1980s. A Class 47 leads a mixed track of 16ton and 21ton mineral wagons with a string of 20ton hoppers behind.

A Class 46 leads a Trans-Pennine express along the main lines.

the introduction of second generation DMUs including Class 150/1, 150/2 and 156 units as well as sectorisation period diesel locomotives for freight traffic.

With so much potential research has been an important part of developing the trains for this layout and while its initial trains play safe there will be more to come in the future.

> *"With so much potential research has been an important part of developing the trains."*
> **MIKE WILD**

Operation

West Riding Power is a very simple layout to operate. The basic premise is that each main line has a storage yard with four tracks in it. These are filled with up to six trains for each direction – multiple trains being accommodated on selected tracks – and these are then run through the scenic section in order to offer a sequence of trains representative of the period.

All locomotives have their lights switched on before departure and speeds are kept sensible so that trains don't speed round the layout in seconds – being only 6ft 6in long it doesn't take long for a passenger train to complete a circuit!

In between the sequence of through trains coal trains arrive and depart from the power station loop using the junctions. These add to the overall picture and we really need at least one more rake of HAA hoppers to provide the continuous movement needed.

All of the signals are controlled with DCC, allowing control of each movement. In the future, with multiple coal trains on the stock list, it will allow us to hold a loaded train at the signal to release an empty train onto the main line prior to the loaded train entering the power station loop. It is this atmosphere which will increase the operational and visual entertainment of what is otherwise quite a simple layout.

The future

This new layout has been a great pleasure to build. Its compact size has seen results achieved quickly through each stage of its construction and the decision to model the 1980s period has been interesting from both a railway infrastructure and rolling stock perspective.

West Riding Power is by no means a fully finished layout and there is plenty of detailing which can be done as well as continuing to develop the stock which completes the picture. We're looking forward to showing this new 'N' gauge layout around the country with its first outings being the 2015 Great Electric Train Show and the Warley National Model Railway Exhibition in November 2015. ∎

A pair of Class 20s cautiously depart the power station loop with an empty rake of HAA hoppers.

Class 58s were rarely seen on coal traffic in the West Riding, but one is still in the fleet for the layout. 58012 draws out of the power station loop with empty hoppers as a HST passes on the main line.

HORNBY MAGAZINE YEARBOOK 8

Forward to 2016

The past 12 months have been busy with new releases, but there are still many models in production. **MIKE WILD** catches up with all the manufacturers' projects and reveals what is still to come.

2016 PREVIEW

2015 HAS BEEN A very satisfying year. New models have continually landed from the main manufacturers and across all three major scales. Hornby has emerged reinvigorated in 2015 after a couple of slow years and since the beginning of the year it has released eight new steam locomotives.

However, Hornby isn't the only manufacturer delivering the goods. Bachmann has delivered three of its own projects in 'OO' gauge together with two commissions while, quite outstanding, is the same manufacturer's commitment to 'N' gauge in 2015 with nine new locomotives reaching the shops during the year.

Dapol too has just begun to regain lost ground with the 'N' gauge 'Grange' 4-6-0 released in August 2015 being its first new ready-to-run locomotive for almost two years. It was swiftly followed by the 'Terrier' in 'O' gauge.

Danish manufacturer Heljan has had a busy year, releasing three 'OO' gauge and two 'O' gauge models including the outstanding Class 05 diesel shunter in 'OO' and the impressive 'O' scale Class 40. There is much more on the cards and 2015 has seen a sea of new announcements take place during the year across all the scales – in fact there hardly seems to be a month go by when a new model isn't announced.

Heljan's 'O' scale model of Brush prototype D0280 Falcon is expected to be released in early 2016.

The Gresley 'J50' 0-6-0T is expected to arrive from Hornby in 'OO' scale during the final month of 2015.

Hornby's model of the Class 71 Bo-Bo electric is making progress towards release in mid-2016.

Hornby is developing the first ready-to-run 'OO' scale model of the Bulleid air-smoothed 'Merchant Navy' for release in 2016. On September 2 1949 35013 Blue Funnel has just passed Winchfield with the Down 'Devon Belle'.
E.C. Griffith/Rail Archive Stephenson.

TABLE 1 - 'OO' GAUGE NEW RELEASES FOR – 2015-2016

CLASS	REGION	MANUFACTURER	EXPECTED
GWR steam railmotor	Western	Kernow MRC	TBA
GWR '1361' 0-6-0ST	Western	Kernow MRC	TBA
GWR '1361' 0-6-0ST	Western	Heljan	2015
GWR '1366' 0-6-0PT	Western	Heljan	2015
GWR '14XX' 0-4-2T	Western	Hattons	2016
GWR '47XX' 2-8-0	Western	Heljan	2016
GWR 'King' 4-6-0	Western	Hattons	2016
GWR '94XX' 0-6-0PT	Western	Bachmann	2016
LSWR 'B4' 0-4-0T	Southern	Dapol	TBA
LSWR '0415' 4-4-2T	Southern	Hornby	2016
LSWR '0415' 4-4-2T	Southern	Oxford Rail	2016
LBSCR 'H2' 4-4-2T	Southern	Bachmann	TBA
SR 'USA' 0-6-0T	Southern	Bauer Media	2016
LNWR 'Coal Tank' 0-6-2T	Midland	Bachmann	TBA
LMS '5MT' 2-6-0	Midland	Bachmann	TBA
GNR Stirling single 4-2-2	Eastern	Rapido Trains/Locomotion	2016
LNER 'J50' 0-6-0T	Eastern	Hornby	2015
LNER 'Q6' 0-8-0	Eastern	DJ Models	2015/2016
LNER 'O2' 2-8-0	Eastern	Heljan	2015
LNER 'V2' 2-6-2	Eastern	Bachmann	TBA
Hunslet 'Austerity' 0-6-0ST	Eastern	DJ Models	2016
Hudswell Clarke 0-6-0ST	Industrial	DJ Models	TBA
Peckett 'W4' 0-4-0ST	Industrial	Hornby	2016
AEC GWR railcar	Western	Dapol	2016
Bulleid 10201-10203	Southern	Kernow MRC	TBA
Class 21/29	Scottish	Dapol	2016
Class 24/1	Various	Bachmann	2015
Class 41 'Warship'	Western	Kernow MRC	TBA
Class 59	Western	DJ Models	2016
Class 68	Various	Dapol	2016
Class 71	Southern	Hornby	2016
Class 71	Southern	DJ Models	2016
Class 73	Southern	Dapol	2015
Class 74	Southern	DJ Models	2016
Class 90	Various	Bachmann	TBA
Class 117	Various	Bachmann	TBA
Class 121	Various	Bachmann	TBA
Class 121	Various	Dapol	TBA
Class 122	Various	Dapol	TBA
Class 158	Various	Bachmann	TBA
Class 450	Southern	Bachmann	TBA
APT-E	Midland	Rapido Trains	2015
Wickham trolley	Various	Bachmann	TBA
L&B 2-6-2T ('OO9')	Southern	Heljan	2016
Baldwin 4-6-0T ('OO9')	Industrial	Bachmann	TBA

'OO' gauge

Even though 15 new locomotives have been completed for 'OO' over the past 12 months, there is still an extensive list of 45 models on the horizon comprising 25 steam and 20 diesel/electric.

All the manufacturers have made new announcements since our 2015 Yearbook survey. Highlights include Hornby revealing its plans for the Bulleid air-smoothed 'Merchant Navy' 4-6-2 and Class 71 Bo-Bo for the Southern Region together with its latest announcement of the Peckett 'W4' 0-4-0ST for release in 2016. Heljan is planning a Great Western Railway (GWR) '47XX' 2-8-0, Hattons of Liverpool a new GWR '14XX' 0-4-2T and Kernow Model Rail Centre a steam railmotor!

Hornby is also nearing completion of its LNER 'J50' 0-6-0T which was announced at the 2015 catalogue launch together with the Adams '0415' 4-4-2T. The 'J50' was due to arrive in the shops during December with the 'Radial' following in the early new year.

Bachmann hasn't shied away from new announcements, adding the Gresley 'V2' 2-6-2, Hawksworth '94XX' 0-6-0PT and Class 117 and 121 Diesel Multiple Units (DMUs) to its list as well as the 450 Desiro. That list is extensive now and consists of 12 locomotives in total across its steam and diesel ranges in 'OO' gauge.

Elsewhere in a follow up to its highly popular collaboration with Bachmann to produce the Great Northern Railway (GNR) 'C1' 4-4-2, Locomotion Models has teamed up with Rapido Trains to offer a ready-to-run model of the GNR Stirling 4-2-2 as the next element of its National Collection in Miniature series. This will follow on from the project to produce the Advanced Passenger Train – Experimental which was nearing completion as this Yearbook closed for press.

Keen to keep up with the times Dapol has stated its plans to produce the new Vossloh Class 68 Bo-Bo diesel-electric with its first models expected to reach the shops during the first quarter of 2016. The manufacturer has also confirmed timing for a number of its 'OO' locomotive projects including the eagerly awaited Class 21/29 for release in the third quarter of 2016, the AEC GWR railcar for the second quarter of the year while the highly anticipated Class 73 Bo-Bo electro-diesel was expected to arrive during November in a multitude of liveries.

DJ Models meanwhile has been working on development of its Hunslet 'Austerity' 0-6-0ST which was undergoing final decoration checks prior to production and release in early 2016. The crowd funded model of the Class 71 Bo-Bo electric was expected to break cover as a first engineering prototype during October with significant progress being made towards its release in 2016. Newly added to the DJ Models product listing in October 2015 is the Class 74 electro-diesel – a class created by rebuilding Class 71 electric locomotives. This is a sensible follow up to the '71' and the '74' is being crowd sourced for funding too.

'N' gauge

Production of new 'N' gauge models has been fluid throughout 2015 with a constant stream of new products for the scale. For the space

Revolution Trains is breaking new ground with its crowd sourced 'N' gauge Class 390 Pendolino by offering it with factory fitted sound.

starved modeller it is rising in popularity again and the manufacturers are delivering an increasingly high standard of new products across locomotives, carriages and wagons.

The total number on the books planned for release now stands as 25 – down three from the end of 2014 and with nine new locomotives being delivered since *Hornby Magazine Yearbook No. 7* was released in November 2014.

The list though is still extensive, although the next new release for the scale is due in October/November 2015 in the shape of the Bachmann Graham Farish BR '4MT' 2-6-4T. Bachmann has been particularly active in reducing its list of 'N' gauge announcements, falling from 12 in 2014 to five in October 2015. These include the GWR '64XX' 0-6-0PT – now at the first engineering prototype stage – the GWR 'Castle' 4-6-0, the London and North Eastern Railway (LNER) 'J72' 0-6-0T and the '4MT' 2-6-4T on the steam front plus a brand new version of the Class 40 for 'N' gauge – a much needed addition to the range.

Dapol is busy too and with the arrival of the 'Grange' it sees to have pulled the stops out for model production with new samples of its 'Schools' 4-4-0, Class 33 and valance fitted 'A4' 4-6-2 all appearing in September 2015 together with a first 3D printed mock-up of the bodyshell for its Vossloh Class 68 in 'N'.

Dapol has also pressed forward with its Class 50 diesel which had been sent for tooling by the beginning of October while its Class 59

TABLE 2 - 'N' GAUGE NEW RELEASES FOR 2015-2016

CLASS	REGION	MANUFACTURER	EXPECTED
GWR '64XX' 0-6-0PT	Western	Bachmann	TBA
GWR 'Castle' 4-6-0	Western	Bachmann	TBA
GWR '63XX' 2-6-0	Western	DJ Models	2016
SR 'West Country' 4-6-2	Southern	Dapol	TBA
SR rebuilt 'West Country' 4-6-2	Southern	Dapol	TBA
SR 'Schools' 4-4-0	Southern	Dapol	2016
LNER 'A4' 4-6-2 (with valances)	Eastern	Dapol	2016
LNER 'J72' 0-6-0T	Eastern	Dapol	TBA
LNER 'J72' 0-6-0T	Eastern	Bachmann	TBA
LNER 'Q6' 0-8-0	Eastern	DJ Models	2016
BR '4MT' 2-6-4T	Various	Bachmann	2015
Hunslet 'J94' 0-6-0ST	Eastern	DJ Models	2016
Hudswell Clarke 0-6-0ST	Industrial	DJ Models	2016
Class 17	Eastern/Scottish	DJ Models	2016
Class 21/29	Eastern/Scottish	Revolution Trains	TBA
Class 23	Eastern	DJ Models	2016
Class 33	Southern	Dapol	2016
Class 40	Midland/Eastern	Bachmann	TBA
Class 50	Midland/Western	Dapol	2016
Class 59	Western	DJ Models	TBA
Class 59	Western	Dapol	2016
Class 68	Various	Dapol	2016
Class 142	Midland/Eastern	Dapol	2016
Class 321	Midland/Eastern	Revolution Trains	TBA
Class 390	Midland	Revolution Trains	2016

The popular Class 40 is to be produced new in 'N' gauge by Bachmann for its Graham Farish range. D261 passes Billingham with a northbound parcels working in September 1967. *Patrick Russell/Rail Archive Stephenson.*

In September the first rapid prototype of the new '00' gauge 'Merchant Navy' from Hornby broke cover.

Dapol has begun moving through its list of products. The 'Schools' 4-4-0 for 'N' has reached the first sample stage.

Heljan revealed the first pre-production sample of its 'O' gauge Class 25 in October.

DJ Models first new locomotive will be the Hunslet 'Austerity' 0-6-0ST. It is expected to arrive in early 2016.

The 'O' gauge 'Warship' by Heljan was at an advanced stage of development in late 2015.

was at the CAD/CAM drawing stage following laser scanning of the prototypes. Both are anticipated for release before the end of 2016. The long awaited Class 142 'Pacer' unit has also progressed with the new engineering samples being evaluated in late 2015 by the manufacturer prior to planned release in the second quarter of 2016.

DJ Models has reported brisk activity on its list of 'N' gauge locomotives with the promised Hunslet 0-6-0ST entering the tooling stage during autumn 2015 together with the Class 17 and Class 23 diesels – all three are planned for release in 2016. CAD/CAM development had reached the final stages for its GWR '63XX' 2-6-0, LNER 'Q6' 0-8-0 and Hudswell Clarke 0-6-0ST in October.

Newcomer Revolution Trains, which uses crowd funding for its projects, has hit the ground running with its Class 390 Pendolino and in September added two new projects to its list in the form of the North British built Class 21/29 Bo-Bo diesel-electric and a Class 320/321 Electric Multiple Unit (EMU) – the first overhead electric to be selected for production as a ready-to-run model. Both models were at the early stages of funding appeals as this book went to press and Revolution Trains is working with Dapol on the Class 21/29 and Rapido Trains for the Class 320/321.

Revolution is also breaking new ground with its Pendolino by offering the first factory fitted sound unit for the British market. Sounds have been recorded from units at Alstom's Longsight depot specially for the Class 390.

TABLE 3 - 'O' GAUGE NEW RELEASES FOR 2015-2016

CLASS	REGION	MANUFACTURER	EXPECTED
GWR '61XX' 2-6-2T	Western	Heljan	2016
Hunslet 'J94' 0-6-0ST	Eastern	DJ Models	TBA
Peckett 'E class' 0-4-0ST	Industrial	Minerva	2016
Class 08	Various	Dapol	2016
Class 23	Eastern	DJ Models	TBA
Class 25	Midland/Eastern	Heljan	2016
Class 42	Western	Heljan	2016
Class 45	Midland	Heljan	TBA
Class 60	Various	Heljan	2015
D0280 *Falcon*	Eastern/Western	Heljan	2016

Hattons has been working on development of its two GWR locomotives including the 'King' 4-6-0. It promises a high level of detail on release in 2016.

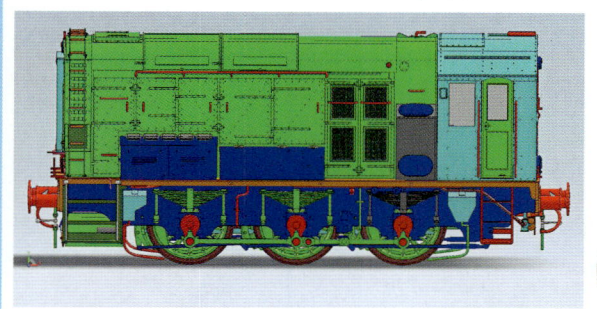

2016 PREVIEW

Having delivered its 'O' gauge 'Terrier' to the shops during September Dapol's next project in 7mm scale is the Class 08 diesel shunter. This is the final CAD/CAM drawing for the model.

Bachmann's next 'N' gauge locomotive release is expected to be the BR '4MT' 2-6-4T. This is the first sample of the new model.

Dapol's eagerly awaited 'OO' gauge Class 73 reached the decorated sample stage in September 2015. Release is expected in November 2015.

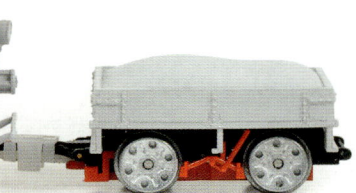

Bachmann has made progress with its attractive – and fully working – Wickham trolley and trailer in 'OO'. This is the first engineering prototype.

Due next in 'O' gauge from Heljan is the BR Class 60 heavy freight diesel. On November 17 2005 60089 *The Railway Horse* heads west near Barnack with an aggregates train. Mike Wild.

'O' gauge

The rise of 'O' gauge has continued with Dapol delivering its first ready-to-run locomotive for the scale in the form of the Stroudley 'Terrier' 0-6-0T. This marked a significant new development for the scale especially considering the price tag of £199.95, which represents excellent value for money for an 'O' gauge locomotive.

Next in line from Dapol for 'O' is the Class 08 diesel shunter which has been accelerated through the design and first sample stages in recent months. Decorated samples are expected soon and the model is pencilled in for delivery to shops in the second quarter of 2016. Factory sound fitted versions will be available.

DJ Models reported that drawing work had been completed on both of its 'O' gauge locomotive projects – the Hunslet 'Austerity' 0-6-0ST and the Class 23 'Baby Deltic' – with the two waiting their turn for the start of tooling work.

Meanwhile Heljan has been working extensively on its collection of planned diesel-electric models with D0280 *Falcon* and its Class 42 'Warship' both due for release in the first half of 2016. However, before that the eagerly awaited model of the Brush Class 60 was due to arrive in October 2015 offering the manufacturer's first sectorisation period locomotive.

Next on the list from Heljan is the Class 25, which has now reached the first engineering sample stage and it is expected to be released before the end of 2016. The Class 45 is also now being developed in readiness for CAD/CAM drawing work to start.

Perhaps the most significant announcement from Heljan came in September 2015 when it revealed that it would be producing its first ready-to-run steam locomotive for 'O' gauge – the GWR '61XX' 2-6-2T. The model is at an early stage, but Heljan says it will be releasing the 2-6-2T in GWR and BR liveries and there is a possibility of producing the earlier '41XX' and '51XX' variants in the future. A full specification had yet to be announced, although a delivery date of late 2016 was anticipated.

New to the 'O' gauge ready-to-run market is Minerva Model Railways – its first project is the Peckett 'E class' 0-4-0ST.

Hornby's Adams '0415' 4-4-2T is making strides towards release in early 2016.

THE HEADLINES

PLANNED 'OO' GAUGE NEW RELEASES			
	2013	2014	2015
Steam:	17	26	25
Diesel:	13	18	20
Total:	30	44	45

PLANNED 'N' GAUGE NEW RELEASES			
	2013	2014	2015
Steam:	15	17	13
Diesel:	15	11	12
Total:	30	28	25

PLANNED 'O' GAUGE NEW RELEASES			
	2013	2014	2015
Steam:	3	3	3
Diesel:	9	9	7
Total:	12	12	10
Overall total:	72	82	79

LNER 'V2' 60931 passes North Queensferry with a Dundee to Edinburgh Waverley express on August 22 1959. Bachmann is producing a brand new version of the Gresley 2-6-2 for 'OO' gauge.
D.T. Greenwood/Rail Archive Stephenson.

Overview

There is still a massive 79 locomotives on the list to be produced and with 2015 delivering 27 new models across the scales and the pace of delivery over the past 12 months could feasibly drop to 50 by the end of 2016. However, there is more to come with Hornby's annual catalogue announcements expected before the end of 2015 and the potential for more projects to be revealed at the Warley National Model Railway Exhibition, the cycle will continue.

One thing is sure – there is a model to attract every taste and certainly in 'OO' and 'N' gauge. 'O' gauge seems set to continue its growth and with Dapol's new 'Terrier' being very well received we can hope that there is more to come for this scale from the manufacturer.

When it comes to 'OO' gauge virtually all the express locomotives have been covered to a high standard and we are now receiving a remarkable collection of earlier locomotives, which represent more ordinary classes and freight engines – the classes which took care of the bread and butter work of the railway.

The model railway world is as exciting as ever and we can't wait to see what our busy manufacturers have in store for us next. ■

HORNBY
magazine

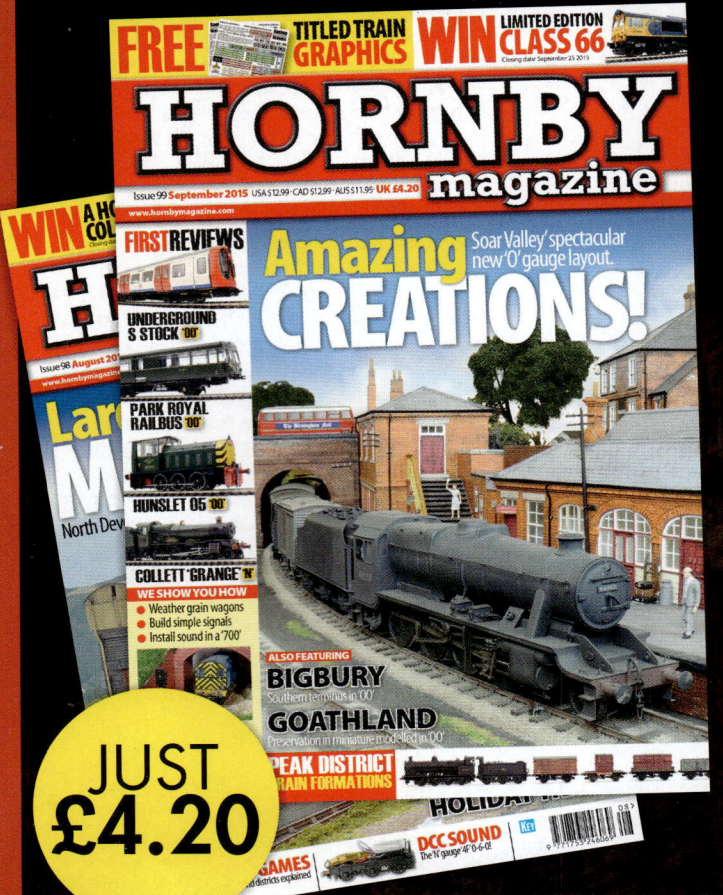

Hornby Magazine takes a unique approach to model railways with both the relatively inexperienced and the seasoned modeller in mind. Unique step-by-step guides offer modellers hints and tips on how to get the most from the hobby. The very best photography and all the very latest news inspire and inform modellers of all abilities. Hornby Magazine is dedicated to promoting this most rewarding of hobbies, introducing it to newcomers and those returning to the hobby. It is written by enthusiasts for enthusiasts - the editorial and publishing team are all active modellers who care passionately about the hobby.

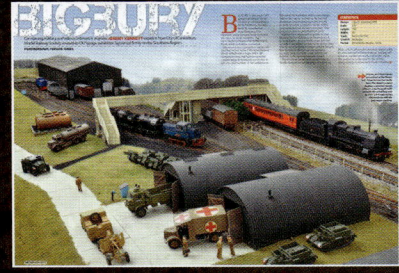

JUST £4.20

Available monthly from **WHSmith** and other leading newsagents

For our latest subscription deals visit **www.hornbymagazine.com**

1150/15

ALSO AVAILABLE IN DIGITAL FORMAT:

DOWNLOAD NOW
FREE APP with sample issue
IN APP ISSUES £2.99
SEARCH HORNBY MAGAZINE

AVAILABLE ON:
- Available on BlackBerry
- Available on kindle fire
- Available on PC, Mac & Windows 8
- Available on iTunes
- Available on the App Store
- Available on Google play

Available on PC, Mac, Blackberry, Windows 8 and kindle fire from **pocketmags.com**

Requirements for app: registered iTunes account on Apple iPhone 3G, 3GS, 4S, 5, 6, iPod Touch or iPad 1, 2 or 3. Internet connection required for initial download.
Published by Key Publishing Ltd. The entire contents of these titles are © copyright 2015. All rights reserved. App prices subject to change. Prices correct at time of going to press.